"Bruno is one of the most creative and thoughtful scientists that I know. In this work, he examines how to use science and technology to make this world a better place—critically important on a changing and increasingly complex planet."

Dr. Ellen Stofan
Former NASA Chief Scientist and
Director of the Smithsonian National Air and Space Museum

"If you liked 'Freakonomics,' you will love this one!"

Najat Vallaud-Belkacem
Former France Minister of Education and Research

Impact Science

The Science of getting to radical social and
environmental breakthroughs.

To my family

To Emma, who shows me
what love is

Foreword

It was 4 am when a voice said, "Yes, you know the *what ... so what?*" in my head. It was late at night, but the sun was over the horizon. There was a bright rainbow ring around it. It was not a dream; I was in the middle of an expedition to Greenland in June. This phenomenon of nighttime with the sun on the sky happens only in summer close to the North Pole. These regions have six months of daylight, then six months of freezing nights in winter. Luckily, it was summer in Ilulissat, the third most populous settlement of Greenland at 4,000 inhabitants. I went for a run (it was daylight, after all) and I had seen on the map that there was a glacier overlook close by.

The streets were full of people: adults going for a walk and kids playing soccer and just hanging out under the sun. I suppose some people save their sleeping for the cold dark months of winter. Being in Greenland breaks many common assumptions, like what is a *day*, what kids should do at 3 am, or how nature behaves. As I left the village and headed towards the overlook point, I remember looking at the sun and seeing a rainbow ring around it. I knew *what* it was. It was the result of an icy layer above in the atmosphere where tiny ice crystals float around, and their collective reflection creates a circular rainbow. Similar to water droplets that make the usual rainbow arcs on the horizon, but these are fully circling the sun high in the sky. Another broken assumption of what a rainbow is.

The overlook point used to be looking at a glacier called Jakobshavn Glacier. Not anymore. I also knew *what* was happening. Because of the warmer weather in the last several decades due to climate change, the leading edge of the glacier has retreated inland[1]. Instead, a beautiful river with icebergs of all sizes was visible. Huge chunks of ice regularly break from the edge of the glacier up the river and float solemnly, moving along slowly. Moreover, as if on purpose to make it more beautiful, right at the edge of the coast where the overlook is, the river mouth is significantly less deep before reaching the open arctic ocean. Like an underwater barrier, it stops the icebergs, stranded or bumping into each other until they melt or crumble enough to continue. Ice is only slightly less dense than water, so it floats, but most

9

of it is still below water. The visible part above the water, the tip of the iceberg, is only 10% of the whole body. The water erodes the ice underneath faster than the air, so sometimes they become unstable and imposingly flip over, showing a smooth blueish surface. When they do that, it is like witnessing the creation of a mountain. Profoundly impressive. I decided to stop for a few minutes to enjoy the view and try my luck at seeing one of those vast icebergs flip around. If you stop, listen, and close your eyes, there is a constant hum of little noises as small pieces of ice fall near and afar. To top it all, as the ice melts, with tiny bubbles of air inside, it liberates air that was trapped millennia ago[2]. One breathes, in fact, ancient air, listening to icebergs cracking and melting due to climate change produced by car and factories far, far away.

"Yes, you know the *what ... so what?*" said a voice in my head. I knew what was happening to the sun rainbow, the origin of the noises, the view of icebergs, their dynamic, what climate change is, that human activity causes it... that is what *facts* and *Science* tell me. I am a scientist and I have studied that. As much as I could explain what was happening, there was a strong voice in my head yelling, *So what?* So what if you know all of that? What difference does it make? What can I do with this knowledge to make a change? I flew here on a plane spewing more CO2 that contributes to climate change. Our group even hired a helicopter to go up the river to the head of the impressive glacier. I did know the impact that this has. What I did not know is what impact this trip could have on me, if any, to help stop climate change. I did not know what impact it may have, for example, to an executive of a natural gas multinational that was also part of the group. Talking to him helped me realize how deeply we all depend on, and demand, the cheap oil whose CO2 emissions we demonize. It painfully unpeels the complexity of implementing the demands climate change science asks. We also had a politician, who later became Minister in Canada. Listening to him helps to understand how complex political leadership is, to position oneself to be democratically chosen and at the same time aim to implement changes that are hard and painful in the short term. I am an astrophysicist; I was not trained to understand economy, politics, or society. On the other hand, my trip mates were not trained to understand the complex chemistry and physics of climate change, or to process the firehose of data we are faced with nowadays. If we are to solve complex real-world problems, we must find a way to merge efforts and skills in the same direction.

Greenland is an exceptional place; it breaks many of your assumptions of reality. Reality is complex: physically complex and socially complex. To understand part of that reality, it might be possible to isolate and focus on a specific part of that complexity. Unfortunately, many of the challenges we need to face require both the ability to understand its facts as well as the ability to actually effect the change we need to do. I could help contribute to the third decimal of how the icebergs melt, or I could try to understand how to incorporate those other messy factors of society, economics, politics… and contribute to create and implement a pragmatic solution, to have a positive Impact. I chose to focus on *impact*. I chose impact science. This is what this book is about.

Introduction

Facts don't change the world, people do. We are creating a world dominated more and more by data and technology, and where fewer and fewer know how to use it. Companies sit on top of vast amounts of data and so do governments, NGOs, and academia. But it is not the data, it is what we do with it.

Historically, we started having scientists seeking and producing most of the data to do research, to publish papers, to *understand*. Understanding has been the core of the scientific revolution, guided by the "free play of the free intellect." Roughly a decade ago, the private sector, especially in Silicon Valley, wanted help making decisions, more than it wanted understanding and research papers. It wanted, for example, to put thousands of small variations of websites to millions of people, and see what combinations work. They were not really interested in understanding why a particular option worked, but on optimizing. On profiling customers. This is why a new breed of scientist—experts in processing data—was born: the data scientists. We could not have enough, so more and more people became data scientists. Today data science is one of the most demanded and rapidly evolving job markets. Yet, it has no formal training, curricula, or even an agreed-upon definition. The skills and tools of this job, heavily subsidized by the private sector's thirst for more results, and the fast cadence of technology, are creating ever better, more complex and powerful tools.

An increasing number of people start to see the problem with this trend focusing on better decisions by mostly getting more data and data-driven decisions. Before, we had scientists in knowledge silos, working on creating better skills and tools in their quest for understanding. Now we have data scientists, creating even better skills and tools in decision making. Data can tell us that a certain genetic mutation in our genes predicts more health care complications and extra cost, though morals (and history) warn us against selectively and genetically breeding and optimizing our kids. Data can tell us that a robot can perform heart surgery more accurately than a person, but few would allow being operated on by only autonomous robots. Data can tell us exactly what message each voter should get so they vote a

15

particular political candidate, but manipulating voters in a democracy this way has poorly understood consequences we only now start to understand... Data is what scientists are trained to manage and understand, and data is what we have exponentially more of, therefore there is an increasing potential and responsibility for scientists to both step in and step out. Step in to engage not only in academics, but also with the consequences and actions. Step out to incorporate and work with experts in other fields and in other realities. For far too long, scientists have built ivory towers where they live in their segmented field of expertise.

For whom is this book?

Getting a grasp of the concept of *impact science* has personally been a long path. When I left academia, it was a difficult choice, and remained for many years a challenging time of uncertainty whether I had done the right thing or not. Looking back at those times I wish I knew that there is a professionally viable, market-growing, and extremely interesting world of science outside academia. I wish I knew leaving academia doesn't mean giving up the "top choice" or that doing so did not mean that I was not good enough. I felt, and was told by a famous political scientist, that society had "invested in me" with a lot of specialized education and I was not using it as I should. That from a public policy perspective, I was a wasted investment. Beyond that, I had no idea what else I could do, where to do it, or how to make that transition happen. This made me feel anxious and frustrated. Moreover, the longer a scientist remains in academia, the harder this transition is. The cost of such transition away from research is facing uncertain rules of your professional value. Losing the hard-earned status one has achieved despite the hardships of academia. These can be very hard moments. I can count more than a handful of colleagues who once were good or really good academics, and faced with this change, they turned into a spiral of medicated depressions, clinical anxiety, and unmet expectations. In the more severe cases, it also meant periods of professional help at mental health institutions or even struggling with suicidal thoughts. So alienating is the way that academia defines

16

success as a scientist. I have since discovered many more people that craved for this change, and found other ways to be a successful scientist while leaving academia, by being what we would call *impact scientists*.

There are two main reasons I wrote this book. One is that I believe impact science is a new concept that is both needed and unknown, perhaps even undefined. I have used the stories of this book to explore this space and the need of more impact science. On both sides, when it is needed and successfully used, and when it could have been used and didn't, or it failed when applied. That is the first part of this book.

The second reason for writing this book is that I wish I could have read back when I left academia. The last section of the book is meant for all those who have an academic background but feel something is missing. They still want to be scientists but haven't yet found their place. Or for their friends and family who want to understand the reason, and path, for such an uncommon and dramatic change from a "normal" scientist. These people curious about impact science wish to engage more with the world beyond academic or public outreach articles. They are tired of the pressures and uncertainties of the academic life and cycle of temporal postdocs, moving countries every two years or so, but they truly don't know how to even think of alternatives.

From Numbers in the Computer Screen to Mud on your Toes

Even before finishing my PhD I had doubts. I loved science, but somehow academia felt less interesting. For most people, myself included back then, science and academia refer to the same concept. You do science working either on basic research or applied research, which mostly correlates respectively with either creating new knowledge within publicly funded institutions or finding applications of the new knowledge at the private sector. That is it. My neck of the woods was basic research. PhD in solar physics at one of the highest regarded institutions in the world, the Max Planck. The message there was clear: here we make top researchers. I still remember the "Career Day" PowerPoint presentation at one of the retreats where the narrative was that only the best get to stay in academia, while saying that staying in academia is the highest goal for scientists: If Option A wasn't working, option B was far below in status and not really an option, but something for those failing option A to consider.

When I finished my PhD, I was proud, but I was also uneasy about the normative academic path ahead. I followed the advice of a friend and interviewed at a major consulting firm (McKinsey). Incidentally this was also the time the European Space Agency did the Astronaut Selection and I was part of the selection process. I remember that during the tests and interviews in both cases, my scientific skills were highly regarded, more even than the scientific knowledge. They liked the problem solving and hypothesis attitude, more than knowing the laws of plasma dynamics. I also cold-emailed the three top academic places in the USA I cloud think of. They were not a continuation of my PhD work, but I also realized once I leave academia, I could not come back, so this was my only chance to give it a last shot. I ended up going to one of these, the rocket lab in Washington DC.

I worked as a postdoc for two years, kept writing papers, going to conferences, and doing occasional public outreach, like organizing global events for the "2009 International Year of Astronomy." Outreach was in a sense the most fulfilling activity, but the research itself was the most exciting and challenging. The discontent with this hard choice grew and I decided to leave at the end of my second year in the postdoc. Leaving this job is one of the most difficult things I have done. It was fascinating to work with satellites and rockets, at a top institution in the world. For someone who comes from a small rural village in northern Spain, it is a long way from home. Moreover, I had no idea what else to do. I felt like I was climbing higher and higher a tall mountain, but it was not the mountain I wanted to climb. To climb the mountain I liked, I had to find it, and I also had to go back down to the lowest part and start again. I applied for, and won, a three months science policy fellowship at the National Academies. My rocket science boss candidly told me he thought it was a mistake if I wanted to stay in academia. I remember being very nervous even asking him to let me go. Academia is very unforgiving, pausing my research and publication cadence could have huge impact in my academic credentials. On top of that, as a non-American I needed his permission to attend the Fellowship while keeping my work visa.

The Fellowship was great to open the eyes beyond academia and into what science policy is. Most of my cohort of policy fellows were in the same spot of recent PhDs wanting to leave academia and not sure how. At the end of the three months I had to go back to the lab. Instead, I told my boss I was leaving. I would lose my work visa, my right to stay in the USA, and it also meant the end of my academic career. I had few weeks to get out the country or find a job, somewhere, somehow. My boss didn't really support that decision, but he said he saw it coming, accepted it, and was keen to help me figure out what I actually wanted.

The USA is known for giving people a chance if you work hard: the "American dream." I also knew that my country, Spain, was deep at the time (2010) in an economic crisis, so I better try out there. Turns out finding a job in the USA is extremely hard even for a (foreign) "rocket scientist." Either they saw no need for one, they saw lack of "real" experience, or they did not want the trouble to get me a work visa. In my extreme, and now embarrassing, naivete, as plan B, I decided to go to Africa and do science policy there. I don't really know what I had in mind, but since in Africa many countries speak French, I signed up to take a French class. It turns out that one of the colleagues in class knew of a new NGO on climate change that was just starting. I interviewed there and got the same answer: no need for a rocket scientist. I did, however, spend a weekend soon after drafting some numbers for the mathematical model the NGO was working on. From my point of view, it was very simple mathematically and it was interesting to plug numbers of something I cared about in the real world. I had a quick call with the executive team, and on the spot they hired me to continue building it: I was to start working at once from Spain, fly for meetings every two weeks, while they began the visa process right away.

I tell the story with some details, because that moment, that arrived from a combination of serendipity and relentless attempts, is the moment I broke the frame I was trapped, as a "scientist." Before this moment, I was labeled as having "no experience" outside academia; after this, I had proven that my skills were valuable in the job market. While preparing this book, I sat down with the NGO boss to ask him why he gave me that chance. It turns out a big part of his trust on my potential was that he also comes from academia, as an engineer. He sees the handicaps many academics have when trying to work outside, but he also sees the advantages if the person manages to adjust. In particular, it was the capacity to talk both in deep technical terms with economic and environmental experts, and also with journalists, politicians, and people with no technical background. From my point of view, I was just leaning on my science outreach experience for this. Just as many academic scientists do, I gave talks about our work to the public. He used an interesting term, "vertical and horizontal vision: Vertical to go as deep or shallow as needed, adjusting the narrative, and horizontal to engage all types of stakeholders, from theoretical mathematicians to heads of state." These are skills that I have worked constantly on since leaving academia, and I believe are core to impact science. The NGO proved not only the breakpoint to leave academia, but also a place I was thrown to learn by doing, combining research, policy, implementation, and marketing. The work we did on the NGO is the story I shared on the last part of the climate change chapter.

21

After two years at the NGO, our data website vendor offered me to go with them to build a new company, Mapbox. They again valued that vertical and horizontal vision. They saw me contributing code to the website and presenting the tool to both a climate change conservative think-tanks, and most liberal researchers. When I also interviewed the Mapbox CEO for this book, he pointed to what I already thought of him, and the USA. He didn´t really care much about the degree, or the academic research; they wanted people that got things done, the things they needed to be done. "Points on the board" he would call it, core to typical Silicon Valley ethos. In fact, since day one, Mapbox has been a mix of artists, philosophers, and graduates from international relations. Only a minority of computer science graduates. I was then the only former academic. Moreover, I realized my academic training, while very useful for the skills I had already used in the NGO, also came with handicaps. For instance, as we were building a project, there were times I realized halfway through that there was a better structure to do it, or a better tool. In academia, it is almost always okay to start over. In academia, the focus is on gaining understanding. In a startup it's always better to deliver it, and then find incremental ways for improvement. The relentless focus on "shipping it" is another Silicon Valley commandment. My work as Chief Scientist at the startup would often involve having to understand new things, but always as a milestone to deliver something. This was uncomfortable at times. It was like running a sprint, and having a double finish line, the one you liked, and the one that matters. As time went by, the company hired a few more academics we had to manage, and I could absolutely feel the same pattern. Just like the NGO boss had seen.

Years later, and having help grow the company from around ten to around one hundred people, I moved to the World Bank. This was the first "Data Scientist" staff position the World Bank had advertised, at the Innovation Labs. When I also met recently with my manager while preparing this book, he highlighted the same pattern of vertical and horizontal vision as a key part of the hiring committee decision. It is not common to see someone with deep technical experience, and strong communications, able to integrate these technical skills into non-technical processes that depend more on strategy, diplomacy, policy. In the years I spent there, I was part of many teams working bridging technical and non-technical aspects of development and technology: Our work focused on how the latest technologic and scientific advances made sense, or not, for development outcomes, in developing countries with developing data. Managing the hyped promises and expectations on both sides. Including my own.

The president of the World Bank, Jim Kim, with whom I could work directly on occasions, has a very interesting background that also reflects this attitude. When he was young, he created an organization, 'Partners in Health', on health care for developing countries which was extremely critical towards the World Bank and wanted to close it as paternalistic and theoretical, too far from the human reality of poverty up close[3]. One of the lessons he shared in staff meetings, and on a Forbes profile in 2016[4], is that "Finance and macroeconomics are complicated, but you can actually learn them. The hardest thing to learn is mud-between-your-toes, on-the-ground development work. You can't learn that quickly. You can't learn that through trips where you're treated like a head of state. You have to have kind of done that before." This echoed very deeply in my idea of impact science. One can learn physics or biology, and these gained skills do have a potential impact in our lives, but to actually realize that impact, one needs on-the-ground experience. You can do some impact science from the lab or from a paper, but one must also go where the intended impact could use some science. I perfectly remember listening to him telling this story, and just a few days later going on a work trip to Dakar, Senegal, to learn about their data science ecosystem, and to help grow it. I remember traveling a few hours to a small village where an innovative NGO, "IamtheCode," was teaching women and girls technology and entrepreneurship. I had so many ideas of open and free software they could use to calculate all kinds of metrics and create data-driven policies. I also remember with embarrassment that most people that attended had no computers let alone laptops, neither they had good data, nor good internet connections. I was right on the value of my ideas, but my approach was useless. I had to mentally switch mode from a paternalistic push, to an iterative dialogue of needs and potential, which continues to this day. To reflect on the words of Jim Kim, the village was too dry to have mud on their unpaved streets, but my feet were dusty while I did my best to help create impact there, on the ground. This is a feeling I have looked for ever since, like the story of Bhutan I shared in the first chapter.

My time as a World Banker was a fantastic chapter that also taught me the timeliness of impact science today. In a world with incredibly efficient digital dividends, it is key to help leverage the latest and most efficient science and technology trends across the globe. Like the circular economy. Like sensors and the internet of things. Like drones. Especially in developing economies. Especially in the constrained context of a developing country, for development goals. Otherwise these digital dividends, would only increase the digital divide and inequality in the world: The developed places, with more funding, more structure, education, and less constraints would absorb the benefits, increasing the divide, or even leveraging it: when a person in Nairobi uses Facebook, gets a ride with Uber, or finds a gig via TaskRabbit, part of the benefits go to Silicon Valley. There is no technical reason it could be precisely in the other direction, where the world would also help drive finance to the developing world, instead to Silicon Valley. That was my goal on one of the projects we did during the time I worked with the World Bank in Philippines and China with regional and city planners. Their strategy and measurement of "accessibility metrics" -how quickly people can get to a hospital, for example- has for long been an incredibly expensive endeavor involving expensive sensors, models, and software. Things like cameras in traffic lights to measure rush-hour locations and times. Meanwhile, any city today has plenty of taxi drivers, or ride sharing apps that can use the software we created to locally map the topology and traffic of their road and street network. Basically using those cars providing rides to people as anonymized traffic beacons. Moreover, much of the software used to develop this solution comes from the open software movement developed by Silicon Valley in their quest for their own apps and services. In a real and beautiful sense these improved data science tools help reduce the digital divide, not just increase it.

There are many other examples of scientists doing this journey from academic science to impact science. The Spanish marine biologist Enric Sala beautifully personifies another such case. He was an academic of marine reserves, environmental protection studies and climate change. After his PhD, in 2000, he got a prestigious position as professor at one of the top academic places on his field, at the Scripps Institution of Oceanography in La Jolla, California. Years later, in 2007, at an even more distinguished institution of National Council for Scientific Research (CSIC), back in Spain. During these years he was fully dedicated to publishing the importance of marine conservation, the effects of climate change and ever-increasing details of the decreasing health of very vulnerable oceans, wild marine life, and coasts around the world. As he told me when we discussed about this idea of *impact science*, he got tired of being the scribe, the witness, of the marine destruction, so he left academia and started a journey driven by the compass of impact, not only knowledge creation. He led a project to create the business model concept of "Fish Bank"[5]. The basic idea being that the reduced profits of not catching fish on these protected areas are vastly compensated by the fish caught overflowing around that area. Moreover, one can include extra benefits setting up sustainable tourism alongside the reserve; that now also harbors more biodiversity. Enric presented this business model with specific simulations and potential pilot sites, but also took into account the economic incentives, financial mechanisms, and politic arguments to align all the incentives from all stakeholders. And indeed, the coauthors of the paper, alongside academics, are a Minister of Foreign Affairs of Netherlands, a World Bank expert, an executive of an insurance company, and an environmental activist. Armed with this multi-stakeholder argument, in parallel, he scoped an action plan. He joined forces with the National Geographic to brand a series of expeditions to pristine oceans. He also had to find a set of donors and benefactors to support the activities financially. These donors and collaborators included the actor Leonardo di Caprio. Enric then used all that economic, financial, narrative, and visual leverage, combined with a thick stack of academic papers, and the sustainability model, to lobby governments to protect the oceans. While it is hard to directly link the protection of seas to a particular advocacy group, this project (called "Pristine Seas") has made twenty-six expeditions, countless numbers of incredibly powerful videos, data for many academic papers, and was also involved in the creation of eighteen marine reserves, and an extra five million square km of sea protected (an area larger than the European Union).

What Bhutan Nuts and NASA Rockets have in Common

In the spring of 2017, I was living in Bhutan, a small remote country enclaved between two giants, China and India. I remember traveling from the closest airport, in Jakar, to the village I was living in, Lignmethan. It is an entire day driving up and down, valleys and mountains passing by, through the "highway"—a mostly unpaved two-lane road with no markings, largely no safety rails on the sides, and boulders and road bumps requiring excellent driving skills to navigate. It is such an incredibly beautiful landscape, and literally one of the most remote places on Earth, due to limited visa permits and long travel times.

I was working for a hazelnut company ('Mountain Hazelnuts'), a for-profit fully foreign-invested social enterprise that provides small trees at no cost to thousands of low-income farmers, to more than double their income reliably for years selling back to the company what they harvest, while the roots of the hazelnut trees protect the land from erosion. The company is based on the coveted "triple bottom line[6]" model of sustainability: for social cause, for profit, and for the environment. It is also a company that loves data and measures everything. I worked with the company for a few months helping to figure out their logistics for the collection of initial harvests from millions of young hazelnut trees, scattered across the country along those infinite roads. I remember being struck by the gorgeous view of the natural landscape, by moments of awe for the beauty and privilege to be there. At the same time, I wondered to myself if it made any sense for an astrophysicist like myself to be doing this type of work.

26

I had studied solar physics as well as completed a doctorate degree to explain magnetoacoustic plasma waves. Following that, I had worked with NASA rockets and satellite missions. My life had not involved many hazelnuts, besides eating them with complete disregard for the paradises they might have come from. Neither was I an expert in logistics, or even in Bhutan. I would have needed some time to locate the country on a map just a few months before.

On the sunny day of my arrival in Bhutan, riding in the car from the airport, I could talk for hours to the driver about the origin of the light that was shining over the landscape and the oddities of the plasma waves up there, still so mysterious to the few people that dedicate their lives to understand them. And to be honest, the driver did love astronomy, and we had plenty of time to burn. It was a beautiful, chatty long ride, but I wasn't there to talk about astrophysics.

I had gone to Bhutan to test the entire concept of this book, the idea that the value of a scientist lies more in their acquired skills and experiences than the facts in their heads. In my years of training as a "professional understander" of physics, I had gained a few potent tools: these included advanced math, modeling, the methods for creating and testing falsifiable hypothesis, and computer coding. These tools proved useful for understanding the distant sun, but—as my hypothesis went—could equally work to offer substantive help closer to home on Earth, for example nut logistics in Bhutan. In fact, such specialized tools I had learned could—and should—work on pretty much any topic measurable with data. The question is, then, how to redirect their usefulness towards maximum positive impact in society versus limiting ourselves to mostly the measurement and understanding of processes.

The company I was working for is extraordinary. Indeed, it is profiled in a Stanford Business School case study due to their broad use of data as part of a strategy for sustainability. I knew I had more than enough material to work with, along with many questions they wanted me to help answer. Having sufficient data to inform strategic decisions is pretty much the rationale behind data science. So I was also wondering if me being in this remote area of the world was just another case of a data scientist working from afar, but within the same framework. My official role was to help create a model to estimate

27

harvest volume and devise the logistical operations to collect it. Yet, I believe there was a significant step beyond the data processing part that made a lot of difference. As we stopped for lunch, I was graphically reminded that implementing scientific solutions in society through data should go beyond just numbers, and it is not just a paternalistic one-way street.

As you approach the door of the restaurant in Sengor (within the Mongar province, atop the last big mountain pass of our trip), you are greeted by the view of two five-foot-long drawings of erect phalluses on the side of the entrance. As you come in, another wooden phallus figure hangs high and erect above on the wall, next to a picture of the king of Bhutan and a calendar. Turns out that in Bhutan, especially in the remote eastern provinces, this is an old Buddhist symbol to protect houses from demons.

Momentarily providing a bit of culture shock, these symbols helped me to start unfolding a deeper understanding of the Bhutanese way of life. The phallus was a conversation starter. I learned about Lama Kunley, who introduced Buddhism to the country in 1499. Other Buddhist practices followed in Bhutan include always going clockwise around stupas (religious stone figures, sometimes in the middle of the road) or the absolute veneration for the sentient life of all animals and insects. The religion forms a strong link to their culture, with a strong respect for nature, low levels of corruption, and an increased feeling of belonging together. The country is, moreover, undergoing a series of profound changes of modernization, from turning an absolute monarchy into a parliamentarian monarchy in 2008, universal healthcare and primary education, or the very recent technology push where TV and Facebook almost arrived at some places at the same time. I also learned that despite great gaps in adult literacy, virtually everyone uses voice messages and pictures with the apps on their phones to communicate, such as WhatsApp or WeChat. The Bhutanese people create a closely linked community with virtually two degrees of separation to anyone else in the country[7]. All of these factors play a crucial role defining reality for the Bhutanese people.

These cultural points might seem outside the scope of my specific work in measuring and assessing hazelnut harvests, at least at first glance. But trying to impose a data-driven solution without such cultural context can definitely backfire. That is the case, just to name an example, of an infamous trend in lake Malawi since 2015. Very well-intentioned global health workers have provided millions of free insecticide-treated nets to prevent malaria from spreading. These are mostly to be dragged to a nearby lake and used for fishing. Not only did that community continue to experience high rates of malaria, people continued to lack sufficient access to malaria prevention, and now they also had toxins in their lake and a dying fish population[8]. Beyond data, perhaps less easily quantified factors such as religion, cultural and social norms, and access to resources need to be considered. Given the growth of data and information available as technology evolves, scientists—who are trained to understand data—are better positioned to help find certain parts of those solutions that will have an impact on reality.

I came to understand very quickly that the remoteness of Bhutan, the character of its people, and the lack of data scientists available to the region would yield my solutions stalled as soon as I left—or worse, void should any tweaks be needed. I was, however, fortunate to have knowledge of previous cases that had failed due to lack of cultural understanding. I was prepared to learn more about the history and religion of the place in which I had just landed. I quickly grasped a need to become familiar with the quirks of driving directions to account for the literacy constraints of some of the farmers and the remoteness of financial institutions, or the tree orchards themselves from roads that trucks could navigate to.

The particular solution we found is not the important part of this book, rather the approach regarding how the scientific skills were used. Over the time I spent there, we quickly identified both the strengths and the weaknesses in our data. We used the regions with the best data to start testing and built a plan to begin completing the data in the rest of the system. We also created a quick prototype of the model to test for blind spots. We found some, such as dealing with non-connectivity zones or being very mindful of the cost of data connectivity. We created a data science program to transfers the skills needed to understand the solution and the tools used. To ease, and constantly test, the knowledge transfer, we established a continued supervised learning among students; I would only teach different parts of the curricula to each student, and then they teach each other the rest while I listen to their lessons. We did some experiments to test travel times, and logistic recommendations. We were at most two phone calls away from speaking directly with someone who knew first hand any direction or location across the country. The Bhutanese are a closely-knit community. By the time I left, we had a first set of logistics recommendations and I left with a fair confidence that the work could continue to improve once I had left.

Focusing on impact meant observing a more complex dynamic as the data tell on paper. It meant making things more complicated; it meant stretching the tools of science to include these constraints; it meant selecting what to train on, how to train, what to build, what tools to develop; and what hypothesis to test and build on. And then iterate and adjust as soon as possible, driven by pragmatism of the messy reality, not dogmatism on top of partial data. It might mean going against what the data says because other factors might be more important, politically or religiously. Impact science means leveraging a scientist first for the skills they have, not the knowledge. Skill-based value, versus knowledge-based value. The knowledge is useful, but more useful, and universal, are the skills learned to create that knowledge a scientist might have.

I remember hearing an interview where the host asked a famous scientist what is the one bit of information, one and only one, you would choose to represent how advanced humankind is. If you had one message to pass on just before ours disappears as a legacy for any future civilization. Or if you had one message to place on an interplanetary spacecraft that will probably survive us before it reaches an alien civilization. Some scientists, if asked, might choose a basic factoid of their field, like the atomic nature of reality, some equations of physics, the axioms of mathematics, or a definition of life. I struggle with this question. It occurs to me if our civilization disappeared, we would forever lose our beloved novels, poems, songs, legends, stories, experiences, religions, or moral values. But not science. Whichever civilization emerged from the ashes, they would recover every single physical law, fact, and theorem of science. The same ones *we* have to the last decimal point. Sooner or later, but exactly the same. Maybe other names and units, but we would recover the knowledge and concepts of nuclear physics, relativity, bacteria, vaccines, or fluid dynamics. That´s the beauty of how universal science is. That body of knowledge would re-emerge identical, like a phoenix, from the right set of skills, like the scientific method. More interestingly, whoever can create the right skills first would create the knowledge that might define a civilization, and in turn further explore the fruits of those skills. Science profoundly influences reality: theory of germs, atomic bombs, the steam engine. Moreover, reality then could be different depending on who discovers what first, and for what purpose. Then it wouldn't be just the facts that defines science's contribution to the world—it would be society that shapes and defines what direction science goes, which in turn shapes society. When I think of that quiz, I wonder how our scientific knowledge, and our world, could have been different, should our history had been slightly different. What more would we know of, because it was important or relevant to the ruling power, and what would we not know? Would we know more about astronomy if the Mayan empire had not collapsed? How would science be if it were not for the European Middle Ages that halted the liberal renaissance revolution of science? How many Einsteins have died victims of hunger, poverty, or bigotry, and their discoveries unknown, because they were not born in the "right" place, at the right time, or with the right skin color, gender, or gender identity?

It is absurd to think science and society do not define, and depend on, each other's potential, even when the facts of science are universal. It is absurd to think science is just about data, discovering facts, and collecting an ever-growing mountain of knowledge wealth. The focus of science should be on its ability to create impact in the society it lives in, that it helps define, and from which it depends, financially and morally. For that we do need the skills of science, and we do need a growing harvest of knowledge, but we also need many other parts of the hard puzzle that makes real impact. Is not only knowledge, it is the whole puzzle. When we succeed, we save the lives of millions, we explore other worlds, we transcend our limits, create new skills, and discover new dimensions of knowledge. When we fail, we roll back the clock of progress, we threaten the environment we depend on, we risk eradicating our own existence.

Moreover, we have historically never seen such cadence of progress, such revolution of technologies, skills and potential, and responsibility of science and technology, as we do today. The chairman of the World Economic Forum, Professor Klaus Schwab, coined the term "[9]fourth industrial revolution" to refer to it. The first industrial revolution was the mechanization using steam engines. The second, mass production using electricity. The third, the digital revolution. The fourth is different; it is not the effect of a revolutionary technology, but the compounding effect of many at the same time—blurring the lines of the physical and digital worlds, machines and humans, or our social contract of work, governance, or identity. In this context, data, data science and science in general play a fundamental role. Not by themselves, not by the knowledge and skills they create, but by the interrelation with other factors. It will be our capacity to understand the impact of data, data science, and science in general, that will help us shape this new world.

To help explore this relation between science and impact, we can use some hard lessons when the gap between understanding the data and creating a positive impact was too large to bridge. I have chosen a few recent cases of such failures. I have also chosen a few recent cases of successes. My hope is that going forward with these, exploring their context and drivers, and raising awareness of this framework can motivate and help create more impact science and more impact scientists.

Missing the Point

As we explore the idea of maximizing science for impact, it is useful to look for examples we can learn from. This chapter explores cases where a developing crisis that has strong scientific underpinnings is unfolding, yet we fail to use these to inform a proper reaction to solve the crisis.

As we will see, a key common thread, is the misalignment of missions. On one side, we have the research incentive where a scientist is trained and rewarded for understanding the process itself on scarce and restrictive funding mechanisms that prioritize the quickest and most likely to succeed fields. On the other hand, we have complex multi-factor multi-stakeholder unknown pathways to solve the crisis, that must include not only research and scientific understanding, but also deal with social taboos, profit incentives, public perceptions, and political capital.

We could, for example, talk about scurvy—a disease that killed millions of sailors on long sea trips and often a substantial percentage of the crew—forcing people to abandon ships, reroute, or cancel ongoing expeditions. On Magellan´s first circumnavigation of the world in 1619-1522, half the crew died from it, and it is estimated many more would have were it not for other causes, likes fights or storms[10]. Today, we know this terrible and widespread disease in sailors results from Vitamin C deficiency. Throughout history, however, the prevention and cure of scurvy has been known and forgotten many times, and consisted of simply eating citric fruits (like lemons or oranges) or fresh meat. In 1747 James Lind, a Scottish physician, scientifically proved that to be the case with a clinical trial, and published it in a few paragraphs within a long and complex book in 1753 (*A Treatise on the Scurvy*). Yet, the prevailing knowledge was that it was a consequence of the sailor´s hard life. Moreover, the logistics and economic pressures to supply fresh fruits to all ships prevented any significant change informed on this scientific knowledge. Meanwhile, the academic leadership remained unscientifically stubborn with lifestyle explanations and against accepting the evidence and historical cures of citric and fresh meat. This included the highest institutions, such as the president of the Royal Academic Society (1772-1778), Sir John Pringle, who blamed scurvy on bad digestion that could be cured drinking malt. Science as a body of knowledge had proven and registered the right answer, but there was no real impact or mechanism to implement a solution. Not until 1795, when a British admiral, guided by the rumors and ineffectiveness of the prevailing treatment, used his authority to order a daily ration of lime juice on his four-month-long trip. The ship arrived with no trace of scurvy, which prompted a Navy-wide policy to secure and supply large quantities of lemon juice. The health improvement of the crew and strategic advantage to the fleet operations played a critical role to the Royal Navy against enemies, that had yet to implement this simple but effective measure. In this case, the scientific corpus of knowledge knew about it, but lacked the power or implementation strategy to drive impact from the knowledge. It could only wait and confirm the effectiveness when the change happened through other means.

We will now explore in detail two cases: the crisis of the AIDS discovery in the USA, and the ongoing global climate change crisis. In the following chapter, we will explore the reality of "Moonshot" thinking, a term that is often related to scientific and technological endeavors that have deep impacts on society. Lastly, we will look at cases where we succeed to solve scientifically-rooted cases. Together, we then explore lessons learned and how we can help maximize the positive *impact*.

When we Look Away, the AIDS Case

How many people need to die before we understand that facts are not enough? One? Ten? A thousand? This is a blunt question to draw attention to the failure in facts alone, even when lives are at stake. Understanding something is, at best, a step in the right direction, but then we must see how to use that vantage point to actually solve the issue. For example, when there is an accident in aviation, there's a committee that investigates to understand how it happened. They spend a great deal of time using many scientific, technological, mathematical, and engineering tools to precisely understand the failure. Once the process ends, they have the facts. Once those are clear, there is another process that ensures it will not happen again. Protocols are changed, new safety harnesses are implemented, policies are changed... as a result, it is rare to see the same type of failure happen again. Air travel gets safer, and we move on with better systems and machines.

The appearance of HIV and AIDS in the USA offers a painful case where we were unable to link facts with action. Where what we called *science* painfully proved to be not enough; our science ecosystem proved clumsy and ill-judged to get beyond the understanding phase, much less to leverage that understanding to save lives across the world, which is arguably more important.

Even today, how much does the average person know about the disease? HIV, or Human Immunodeficiency Virus, attacks the body's immune system, eventually destroying its defense mechanisms against even minor infections. This health condition is still seen with stigma by many, associated perhaps with risky or immoral behavior. There is also misunderstanding about its transmission. Today, while there is no cure, through consistent and sustained treatment, a person living with HIV can achieve a level of virus in their body that is undetectable by most standardized blood tests. At this point, it becomes virtually impossible to spread the virus and an individual can reach a life expectancy approaching that of the general population. When left untreated, the HIV infection can lead to AIDS disease, or Acquired Immune Deficiency Syndrome, which is fatal.

HIV is now known to have come from Africa, probably around present-day Kinshasa, Democratic Republic of Congo. It was probably the combination of the colonialism that brought development and an influx of foreign workers. Prostitution and sexually transmitted diseases helped transmit the original infection around the 1920s, probably from the bite, or meat, of a simian infected with the virus where HIV mutated from. With a long incubation period of a decade, and during which one can transmit the disease, the virus silently spread below the medical radar for years. It is suspected to have traveled far via expat workers. For example, it probably arrived in Haiti around 1966 or earlier. In Norway, in 1976 a sailor, his wife, and one of his daughters died from the HIV he contracted while sailing in Africa years prior. In 1977, a Danish physician died from AIDS after having worked in Zaire for years.

In the early decades, HIV hit most sub-Saharan Africa, but the USA in particular saw a rapid growth and spread, particularly among homosexuals. There are several hypotheses for this. Some factors include that Port-au-Prince, the capital of Haiti, was a popular cruise gay destination for Americans. Studies of those times estimate several factors conflating on the spread of this epidemic in the gay community: an average of twelve different sexual partners per person per year, the high rate of infection with gay sex, and the coincidence with a nascent liberation and concentration of gay communities, especially in San Francisco and New York. Intravenous drug users were also hit hard with a high rate of infection by the practice of sharing needles. Many European countries had public health policies such as programs to offer needle exchanges, while the USA mostly deferred action nor acknowledged awareness[11]. Eventually, the general population outside these high-risk areas were affected. Mothers passed HIV to their babies, the blood bank supply—without capacity to detect the problem—got infected from affected donors, and then passed it on to people that underwent medical operations. Hemophiliacs (people with limited ability to stop bleeding when cut) were a special case. At the time, a new life-saving product, 'Factor VIII', was invented by which they could have almost normal lives if they received regular transfusions. This Factor VIII was produced from donor blood. Every person with

38

HIV that donated blood contaminated the doses for several people's worth of Factor VIII. 10,000 people are estimated to have received HIV from this source alone[12].

Unfortunately, it took many years to acknowledge the nature of the pandemic, to discover the virus, and to develop the type of lifesaving treatment individuals living with HIV have today. When the virus appeared in the United States during the early '80s, it was not well understood and was dubbed the "gay plague," as the homosexual community was first seeing the most cases. With rampant social stigma and discrimination against the homosexuals, the matter was not taken seriously.

The purposeful avoidance of a focus to find a treatment for the devastating illness may have hindered understanding on how it spread. It shouldn't have taken so long. As early as 1982, researchers knew there was something in the blood bank supply that was causing individuals to acquire AIDS later on. Early that year, the CDC, Center for Disease Control and Prevention in Atlanta, Georgia (the highest U.S. public health authority) had the facts: AIDS was a mortal disease that was spreading at alarming rates and had been proven to be transmitted through blood and sexual contact, including via products for hemophiliacs.

Unfortunately, 1982 is also the same year of a now infamous recording at a White House press briefing. President Ronald Reagan's Press Secretary, Larry Speakes, mocked a journalist for being interested in how the White House was addressing the spread of the then-dubbed "gay cancer" or "gay plague."[13] At the time, the disease was seen as a joke to those in power, who threw innuendos and insults at the problem. And so, for several years, HIV remained mostly unspoken, unaddressed; yet spreading across people. Discrimination won out. Bureaucratic and political red tape and economic interests trumped public safety, while jokes were made at the highest policy levels. Research funds and scientists were disincentivized from dedicating themselves to this taboo topic. [14]New cases were mounting at exponential rates, and now via blood transfusions to the general population from infected donors. Then, it became more broadly known as an important public health issue, since it was affecting a wider population. The public stance changed, but no new funding was made available.

In 1985 the director of the CDC laboratory dedicated to this new epidemic, Don Francis, drafted the first plan. Don is an epidemiologist who had worked on containing the cholera epidemic in Nigeria in the early 1970s, the smallpox epidemic in Yugoslavia in 1972, and the 1976 Ebola epidemic in Sudan. He understood the severity of the situation and the expensive cost of a program that could work to prevent even more deaths. He also understood the even higher cost, economically and in lives lost, of not addressing the epidemic with full force as soon as possible. His proposal, called "Operation AIDS Control" asked for $40 million per year (~$100 million adjusted for inflation), educational programs for gays on safe sexual relations, for drug users on safer practices, clinics, research, and an unequivocal political public acceptance of the crisis. Not only it got denied, but the response was to "look pretty and do as little as you can." In fact, Don's boss, the Director of the CDC and medical doctor James Mason, was part of an administration than wanted as little new funding and talks about the gay disease as possible. Years later, in 1992, at a conference where Mason was defending from criticism by experts that the government's AIDS campaign was too vague and ineffective, he also stated that "there are certain areas which, when the goals of science collide with moral and ethical judgment, science has to take a timeout." Before joining the CDC, from 1970 to 1975, Mason had been the director of the hospital services of the Mormon church, whose faith forbids same-sex sexual behavior. After the CDC, Mason, from 1994 to 2000, served at the general authority of the Mormon church, the "Second Quorum of the Seventy." It is fair to say that Dr. Mason had pressures from many sides. From the administration he believed in, from his culture and faith, and from his scientific and operational training in public health.

At the same time, prominently in San Francisco, activists, leaders of the gay community, and scientists collided with heated arguments on how to deal with the spreading epidemic. Some of the scientific recommendations wanted to close bathhouses, interview, record, and test whole communities, and promoted avoiding gay sex until more research could inform how to have safe sex. On the other side, gay business owners and community leaders wanted to protect their culture and personal freedom of the liberties they had just won[15].

As pressure to investigate the epidemic mounted on top of the rapid increase of deaths and new infections, the incentives swung to the other side, and competition among researchers for patents and name recognition caused further delays. It was clear that a Nobel Prize was at stake. This competition included suppression of data and a reluctance to share data, isolated virus strains or protocols that could give the competing teams competitive advantage[16]. Meanwhile, the facts were clear: people were continuing to be infected and the deaths kept rising.

So, how many people needed to die before the facts were acted upon? It was not until 1985 when blood testing was finally introduced based on scientific recommendations. At least 7,000 people had already died, and many more became infected of an incurable virus before we started to implement the scientific recommendations that experts had called for. Being an infectious disease, the direct and indirect infections from the delaying action had an exponential effect. As described by San Francisco Chronicle journalist Randy Shilts in his book *And the Band Played On*, the AIDS crisis marks a very painful moment in science history. Facts were mounting on the spread of the disease. And it had been spreading not only among stigmatized or marginalized individuals such as the gay and drug using communities, but also among infants, children, and adults who had received blood transfusions during surgical operations, or hemophiliacs requiring regular transfusions. Public perception grew alongside new cases, and it was also accelerated whenever a celebrity like a famous actor or singer declared they were infected. People like Rock Hudson, an American actor who died in 1985, and who was a personal friend of the USA president. This was not an invisible unexpected "black swan" of later consequences, but a huge obvious "Grey Rhino": it was a very visible problem coming in fast, which many in positions of power or influence refused to react to. The science was clear, but experts were just not getting through.

Fate had it that AZT, the first treatment approved in 1987 for HIV, was actually discovered in 1964 but shelved since it proved inert on the mice cancer it was researched for. Not until 1985 it got picked up as a potential treatment based on the overlap between HIV research and the AZT research decades earlier.

It would be too easy to claim that politicians should have listened more to the scientists, and less to the for-profit interests of private blood banks. The scientific recommendations of the time required spending a lot of money to apply a test, which had proven only partially effective. It would also be too easy to say we needed louder voices and clearer messages from scientists. When I look at this crisis, my mind wanders instead towards what else the scientists could have done to understand and *adapt* to the challenges of the situation at hand. For example, what would have happened if years before someone with a strong impact science training would have made its way to the White House Cabinet as Scientific Advisor? What if better data collection and scientific support protocols had been in place? If famous people, not only scientists, would have spoken earlier about solving the issue? There might have been opportunities for scientists in the United States to collaborate and share information with scientists in France, who were making more progress towards a treatment for HIV. There were no incentives to maximize that. What might have happened if scientists had stepped outside of their immediate roles and dedicated more funds to a widespread communication, information sharing or ideation strategy? What if they understood how to deal with the cultural role of the gay baths when most its users and owners refused to close them, despite being at the center of the infection transmission hub? These aspects were not within the scope of their research, or communicating their research findings, but they do run parallel and are critical to deriving a positive impact from that knowledge. I do think of what needs to change in the science community, or in the role of scientists at for-profit industries, in government, in journalism, so that this doesn't happen again. As painful as it is to acknowledge, discrimination against people who had acquired HIV or AIDS delayed progress on the disease.

Unfortunately, we don't need to go too far back in history to find other examples of other global challenges with clear scientific underpinnings. A number of urgent global issues could be better addressed if science and scientists were more effective at moving their messaging beyond facts and figures. Scientific facts alone don't change the world. *People* change the world. People, leveraging all aspects involved, from science to culture, strategy to politics, economics to religion. We can, for example, look at climate change.

The Witness Paradox of Climate Change

Climate change is another of these long-called failures, or as Michele Wucker called it, "Grey Rhinos[17]" cases. Everyone knows what a grey rhino looks like. This one is even charging at you with known consequences of inaction, but we see it coming and do nothing, as we keep seeing it coming. It is a case where the scientific emphasis is mostly siloed on understanding the processes, without having it turned into meaningful change in practice. At this point, there is no reasonable doubt that human activity is pumping out greenhouse gases, like CO_2, that are disrupting the climate systems at a global scale. This disruption has negative effects on the landscape, the oceans, life in general, and our society and support systems like agriculture. The frequency and intensity, and costs, of extreme events like floods and droughts, have increased and will continue to do so. The average temperatures in the surface will keep rising, putting more stress on our health, food production, livelihoods, and lives. Eventually this stressed system might pass a threshold of no return, deemed at around two degrees Celsius of warming above the Industrial Revolution time. At this stage, instead of adjusting by being warmer, the whole climate system changes and the impacts are not anymore incremental but radical. We can measure this, we can understand how and where these changes will happen. We know where these gases come from. We can even model the effects of having more gases. As the scientific community has put forward, if we want to minimize the consequences we must, right now, massively reduce our CO_2 emission (it's too late to avoid repercussions completely, we can only reduce the impact).

The strategy of reducing the emissions is called "climate change mitigation." There is also a parallel track, called "climate change adaptation" which is to accommodate for the climatic changes we already see, and the ones we will likely see incoming. Climate change adaptation is, in fact, increasingly important as we prove unable to mitigate. The key concepts here are that we understand that climate change is caused by humans, and that we can probably stop it with mitigation, and in any case some degree of adaptation is needed. Adaptation is also increasingly more expensive as we fail to mitigate.

Through the discovery and popularization of climate change, mitigation has been the first priority, while adaptation was mostly being seen as a measure of dealing with the failure. Al Gore, in his 1992 book *Earth in the Balance*, called adaptation a "kind of laziness, an arrogant faith in our ability to react in time to save our skins." On top of that, the private sector has always been seen as the culprit of climate change, the target of those demands to stop pollution. As if it were an external entity just pumping out gases, deaf to science. The scientific community in those early days was essentially dedicated to explaining with ever increasing detail the processes of how the private sector is putting us into deeper trouble, how we ought to stop pollution immediately, and how not even adaptation would work. Adaptation was like a person buying bigger clothes as they failed to mitigate eating more cakes. And we kept emitting more, and the effects of the climate change took its toll on more land degradation, less agricultural crops, more disasters... in fact, affecting those who were most vulnerable in developing countries, that also were emitting least. A double injustice. And we kept writing papers. Scientific careers fully dedicated to dissecting these destruction processes. Whole UN bodies to make crystal clear what was the science and how proven it was. From the individual and research community perspective, scientists were achieving their objective: peer-reviewed papers, citations, tenure, increased basis for their claims and cries... from the global perspective, the world kept mostly on the so-called "business as usual," and we still are flying towards the finely calculated and quickly approaching threshold of $2\,^{*}C$ degrees above which things will get disproportionately worse.

In early 2010, as the evidence of climate change mounted, an increasing group of people started calling for addressing the role of the private sector beyond an easy blame of being the source of the devil pumping of CO2. Yes, the private sector is responsible for most of the emissions[18], but virtually every gram of it is a service or a product that is sold, it represents the employment of millions of people, the very fuel that powers our increasing well-being in society. As much as it is

46

vilified, we need it to produce our food, move things and people back and forth, even fly to the conferences we talk about how much CO2 that is. As part of our social fabric of well-being, we simply cannot shut down today all factories, ground planes, and close mines, as the science shows we physically need to if we want to abate climate change. Furthermore, if given the choice of the same product or service at a higher price in return for a less environmental footprint, most of us won't want to pay, or can afford, the extra premium cost, like when given the choice of an ecological fruit versus a standard one. And the opposite is true: wealthier people and societies that could afford paying more to have a similar but more sustainable lifestyle, have lifestyles that instead pollute more, like when buying an extra car for convenience, instead of pushing for better public transport.

As much as it pains to realize this, currently our socioeconomic status is substantially coupled to environmental unsustainability. Decoupling this will need much more than papers, or books, saying that much. Part of it is collective behavior, habit inertia, and lack of incentives to change. Just like most of us don't really change our behavior after our dentist tells us to floss more, our doctor to eat less fat, or our bank to put more into our savings account. Climate change is not a political priority, as it is not something that will make people change their vote in an election. On the contrary, the candidate who promises less subsidies to oil, or more taxes to offset carbon, will probably lose votes, especially from those who would lose their jobs. But even more difficult, many people simply cannot afford to buy the more expensive healthier food or cannot afford to upgrade their old and oil-thirsty car to go to work.

The private sector and adaptation, a historical double devil, could in fact play a substantial role in finding its own double positive role. They could cover most of the finance, either by protecting their own assets or supplying chains that in the future would suffer. If chocolate beans don't grow, there is no chocolate industry. Additionally, private finance has a designed capacity and expertise in balancing risks and investments, and thus would tend to put venture capital in the emerging markets of climate-resilient products and services. There is a solid strategic angle to engage and articulate in detail the relation of private sector and adaptation to climate change, not only to start discovering solutions, but also as we aim to shift or replace several pillars of society, and many livelihoods—of course, as a parallel track of mitigation efforts. Today, this is part of the common narrative. Today, there are many efforts, articulated strategies, and dedicated funds on both the mitigation side and on the adaptation side, and also engaging the private sector as key partners. But back in the 2010s, the private sector and adaptation were mostly two big taboos, especially in scientific debates. I remember attending the private sector side-event at one of the UN key conferences on climate change, "COP 17" in Durban, South Africa. The keynote speaker at a session, a CEO from a multinational, said that "we are not here to 'pay the bill' of climate change, we are here to work together on pragmatic solutions we can start implementing now." These were also the pillars of the "Global Adaptation Institute," or GAIN, the NGO where I landed in 2011 right after dropping my very academic postdoc.

The biggest scientific lesson I learned in my time at this NGO is that the scientific narrative could be very patronizing and uncompromising with pragmatism. We should do what scientists tell us, because if we knew what they know, we would do as they say. This attitude of a typical scientist, I saw, is the case even when we engaged all stakeholders on the same table: a research scientist, a finance or labor minister, and a CEO of an oil company. We are all in it together, and waving a fact flag or a research article won't work to confront the livelihood, the votes, or the cultural attitudes of people. At GAIN we invited the ten most cited and published academics on adaptation, as well as CEOs from many industries and representatives from governments, civil society, and other NGOs. We spoke, for hours and days and weeks, and our job at the time was to find common anchors of understanding between these stakeholders. We had scientists telling us about the bluntness of the needed reductions. How deep and quick these need to be. How much more research, and research funding, was needed. How dire the consequences were of not listening to the facts they found. We had government officials telling us about our dependence on oil in the labor market or in transport, as well as their lack of finance for this, or political budget to push this agenda up. We had companies who agreed on the needed change but the inability, or lack of incentive, to turn around whole industries on their dime, while covering the demand for their products and the competitive markets. Any increase of pricing would simply turn the consumer towards the competitor. We had groups denying the human-made nature of climate change but agreed on the need to increase resilience. Facts are facts, but the world is what it is. Facts don't change the world, people do. And people are... complex. Any truly transformative solution would need to include all these stakeholders, working together. Somehow.

Our team leveraged the input for social scientists, economists, strategists, innovation, and ideation experts. The result of this process, our flagship product, was to distill the idea into a simple ranking, that unfolds into a matrix of Vulnerability and Readiness, that further unfolds into a detailed view for each country and for each factor. The ranking worked really well to start a conversation of who is up, or down, and then wonder why. The matrix was used to convey a holistic view that any solution had to deal with the natural vulnerability but also the societal readiness to do something. The last layer, the deepest one, aggregates and combines the full complexity of more than 30 variables, for more than 15 years of data, for more than 170 countries in the world for which we had enough data. This "onion-layered" approach proved key to engage everyone into an iterative process to improve it, showcase it, and draw attention not only to the issue, but also to start bridging understanding into solutions, and what impact, from who, and how, would see what effect.

While our efforts and team were small, I know of no other initiative that had such a positive and engaging response when presenting the very same tool and recommendations to research scientists, climate change deniers, journalists, the CIA, the World Bank, ambassadors, logistics companies, investors, and a long list of stakeholders we engaged. As a scientist myself, just out of academia, I felt incredibly empowered to be able to engage deeply with such a variety of actors. The model that calculated those numbers pulled from many sources and amounted to a few million data points, but it was mathematically trivial compared to the solar magnetoacoustic plasma waves I had done a few months before. It also felt incredibly more meaningful to the world than that basic research, as important as it is to understand the sun. It was precisely my advantage to operate mathematically quickly and swiftly that allowed our meetings to move fast, as we could see, or estimate, the impacts of the proposed changes in the model, often in real time, while I tweaked the code. Paradoxically, math was important, but it was only a very small subset of other factors much harder to evaluate and plan, and for which I had much more to learn and listen, like finance, culture, history, and politics. The anchor was not the science, the anchor was the positive impact we all wanted in society. We were solving for *impact*. My role was the part of that impact that can be helpful with the facts and, more importantly, the skills that scientists learn. My role was to be the impact scientist, although I only realized that many years later.

The Uncomfortable Truth of Moonshot Mindset

We often hear the phrase "Moonshot mindset" referring to huge leaps of discovery and progress, driven by the purest sense of exploration, curiosity, and daring attitude to the unknown—to the difficult options few even consider trying. It refers to the attitude that led us to land people on the moon, a promise made when it seemed too crazy, too impossible. In researching this book, many referred to places with this shared attitude, like Google's "Moonshot Factory" like Mecca's of Science. The more I investigated it the more I realized there was much more than what it seems. In fact, this chapter is dedicated to unfolding the somewhat uncomfortable truth of the "Moonshot mindset" that led us to the moon. A mindset where values seldom associated with this attitude were key for achieving the lofty goal.

We went to the Moon due to a deep political and financial commitment, an obsessively focused project management attitude, with no space for any unaccounted exploration, but for achieving the stated goal. In that sense, the Moonshot mindset had a precursor in the discovery of the atomic bomb just a few years early, and a shared political and strategic common background. There are important lessons to learn when looking at how we first achieved the Bomb, then then Moonshot, and what we can learn about when doing science driven by impact.

The Bomb

If one had to summarize the twentieth century in few key events, it would surely have both World Wars, including the Nazis and the atomic bomb; and the Space Age when, for the first-time, humans left our planet and explored the cosmos. Two of these events—the atomic bomb and the moon landing—have deep scientific and technological underpinnings. The atomic bomb culminated years of intense and focused basic research on nuclear physics, with the Americans fearing what the Nazis would do if they got it first. It required a huge cooperation between scientists, engineers, mathematicians, and other experts. It involved both basic research and applied physics in full synchrony between each other, and against the unknown progress of the enemy. Americans had to beat the Nazis.

In August 1939 the famous physicist Leo Szilard wrote a letter, which Albert Einstein signed as well, and they sent it to the USA president. It argued that with the recent discoveries in physics, a radically new and massive bomb was possible. One that could swing the war in one stroke. Theoretical physics was living a revolution pulling the threads of the revolutionary findings of a new field: quantum physics. At the same time, the Second World War had just started after Nazi Germany invaded Poland. As the war became more complicated and dominated by technology progress, progress in theoretical physics kept coming closer on how to conceptually release the immense power of breaking an atom. In 1941 President Roosevelt, advised by Vanebar Bush, decided to approve and give very high priority for a program to develop the atomic bomb, the "Manhattan Project."

Vanebar Bush was an engineer and prolific inventor who found himself increasingly involved in the management of scientific institutions. He was essentially the first scientific advisor to an American president. During his long career he was Vice-President of the Massachusetts Institute of Technology (MIT), and Acting President of the National Advisory Committee for Aeronautics (NACA—the predecessor of NASA). In 1941, the year of the letter by Dr. Szilard, President Roosevelt created the Office of Scientific Research and

Development (OSRD), which would grow to coordinate six thousand American scientists on how to create and apply science to war efforts. It is in the context of the OSRD that the efforts to develop the atomic bomb were placed and prioritized. After the war, in 1945, Bush wrote a memo titled *Science, The Endless Frontier*, outlining his vision of a national strategy for science, including the importance of the "free play of the free intellect." This memo also conceptualized a public funding mechanism that later became the National Science Foundation, or NSF. The NSF today has an annual budget of seven billion dollars. It is worth noting that under his guidance, the OSRD produced an incredible amount of scientific progress, both as academic knowledge, and applications (and both for defense and civil contexts). Yet, the OSRD strategy—in practice the USA Wartime Science Policy—was fundamentally opposite to the science strategy of his later peacetime Science Policy memo. In fact, the person chosen to direct the Manhattan Project and the laboratory that were to invent and build the first atomic bomb, the physicist Robert Oppenheimer, also had the same approach to manage science.

Dr. Oppenheimer was a theoretical physicist in charge of a very difficult problem, with a very tight deadline. The Moonshot before the Moonshot. Getting to the finish line was the only priority, and time was the scarcest resource. Dr. Oppenheimer had to balance the exploration of new ideas, with exploitation of known ideas. Everything was secondary to getting the bomb, including research, but it was also clear that much basic knowledge had to be created even to figure out if such a weapon was possible. The whole team had to manage creating new hypothesis, testing them in experiments or models, and then applied and refine them, but only if they brought the team across the finish line. He was able to manage a wide range of issues, from interacting with the Department of War (now Department of Defense) and their military mindset, to participating in the theoretical meetings to choose which hypothesis to investigate, which engineering model to build, or who to hire, or what to buy to get the answer faster. The menace of a Nazi global domination put aside all other considerations, including academic worthiness or even personal convictions.

In parallel, a team of Allied scientists—the Alsos Mission—started shadowing the war frontline progress in Europe, confirming the unlikely advantage of the Germans getting the atomic bomb. It soon also became clear that the design was not the only challenge, but also where to get the right kind of uranium, and how to prepare it and enrich it to be useful. This also meant that controlling uranium fuel mines was a defense mechanism, and that creating uranium processing facilities was a technological barrier to handle. Germany, Japan, and the Soviets were confident such a combination of research, engineering, and logistical challenges placed the atomic bomb beyond the scope of the ongoing war. Oppenheimer was committed to ensure Americans had it first, and as soon as possible.

Progress moved quickly, and they were successful in July 1945, exploding the first atomic bomb, nicknamed "Trinity," in New Mexico (USA). By then, the defeat of the Nazis was almost finished, and Hitler had committed suicide in April that year. The prime reason to beat the Nazis in the atomic bomb was already off the table. The bomb was nonetheless used a month later in Hiroshima, and another one in Nagasaki. These bombings made the existence and might of the new kind of weapon publicly known, and Oppenheimer a cover-page hero for leading the project. However, ten days after the Japanese attack, he went to Washington DC to argue directly with the head of the Department of War against using atomic bombs. His position against nuclear warfare grew alongside his fame, which he used to lobby for non-proliferation of atomic bombs. Oppenheimer was once a member of the Communist party in the USA and with very liberal views at the time. Throughout his life he had to endure investigations, and after the war was over, and his pacifist views openly clearer, he had to suffer public humiliation and revocation of his security clearance. As the cold-war era settled in, any stance or doubt about the national politics was the target of anti-Soviet warmongering politicians. This volatile relation between the scientists at the core of the military progress, and the normative mindset of the American Cold War forced Oppenheimer to confront many accusations. The father of the American rockets, Wernher von Braun, testified in his defense that in "In England, Oppenheimer would have been knighted."

Oppenheimer spent his later years increasingly concerned with the potential dangers to humanity by scientific discoveries. He became a global activist and lecturer for this cause, and for the broader role of science in society. His lectures and publications gained worldwide attention and awards across Europe. France made him an Officer of the Legion of Honor in 1957, and Britain elected him as a Foreign Member of the Royal Society in 1962. In 1965, President John F. Kennedy awarded him the prestigious Enrico Fermi Award, rehabilitating his figure and public recognition. He died four years later. Oppenheimer was a brilliant scientist who was able to master academic skills during his early career. Someone who faced the threat of fascism by fundamentally assisting the Allied effort, breaking the image of scientists with their heads in the clouds, and that theoretical academia was far from real-world applications.

The struggles of the father of the American atomic bomb discovering it, and working to shape a positive outcome from it, has a striking similarity on the Soviet side. They did not have a similarly sized or prioritized "Manhattan Program" but they closely followed, and spied, on them. After Hiroshima and Nagasaki, the Soviets realized they had to catch up to the clear military advantage of the bombs. They tried to replicate the Manhattan Project path of discovery as much as possible, and also gathered their best scientists. One of key ones was the physicist Andrei Sakharov.

Dr. Sakharov was the son of a physics teacher and pianist, and grandson of a prominent lawyer who advocated for social awareness and human rights. Young Sakharov studied physics in Moscow, was forced to move due to the war, and finished his degree in Ashgabat (today's Turkmenistan). Sakharov then did his PhD in a prestigious theoretical physics institute back in Moscow. Soon after getting his doctorate, he joined the post-war soviet atomic program, a move that proved fundamental to the Soviet progress. He conceptualized the design of how to make their atomic bomb work. In fact, the most powerful nuclear device ever detonated, the Tsar bomb in October 1961, with more than 3,000 times the power of the weapon dropped on Hiroshima, used what is today known as "Sakharov's Third Idea." Sakharov saw the strategic disadvantage upon the Soviet empire if only

Americans had the bomb. He helped advance military might of destruction, but in parallel he also advocated for non-proliferation, peaceful uses of atomic energy, and a ban of atmospheric nuclear tests, which had many more harmful consequences than subterraneous tests.

Especially after his involvement with the Soviet nuclear atom, Sakharov was an activist of science progress and against pseudoscience. At the time, the biologist Trofim Lysenko was pushing the idea that plants could change species when given the right treatment and rejected the concepts of genes. Stalin embraced this "Lysenkoism," which aligned with the communist ideals of equality and rejected the deterministic nature of races and generic fate. Genes and evolution in animals are still today rejected on some small Christian communities in the west, but not to the extent Soviets did with agriculture. This official stand held research progress, while the rest of the world developed the skills and knowledge to improve their seeds and crops. It also meant that from 1920 to 1964, more than 3000 pro-genes scientists in the Soviet Union were fired, sent to prison, or even killed. Sakharov used his political weight to actively campaign against Lysenkoism and the prosecution of "genuine scientists." In 1968 Sakharov wrote an essay that advocated for diplomacy and trust instead of the intensification of the Cold War arms race that would aggravate the consequences of a potential arm conflict. He was banned from military research for this and forced to go back to civil research. He became a political activist, openly defending peace, democracy, and human rights. In 1975 he was awarded the Nobel Peace Prize but was banned from traveling to collect it in Oslo. In 1980 he was forced to exile to Gorky, a Soviet city off-limits to foreigners. In the next years he got more awards for his humanitarian activism, and in 1985 the European Parliament established an award in his name for outstanding contributions to human rights. In 1986, under the perestroika reforms, he was allowed back to Moscow. In 1989, he was elected to the new Parliament and died in December of that year.

Both Oppenheimer and Sakharov lived a parallel scientific compass of values. They both played fundamental roles in making the most destructive bomb humans have known, and they were at the center of the scientific, political, and military realities of their time. They both became increasingly concerned with the effect of an accelerated scientific progress. From the vantage point of time, it is too easy to morally judge their contributions to the military and their responsibility to millions of deaths directly and indirectly through their creation. What is clear is that they were both, especially on the latter parts of their lives, extremely conscious and engaged with the moral responsibility of science, its role beyond data-driven progress, and the broader relation of co-dependence between science and society.

Besides creating the atomic bomb, nuclear physics these decades also created the technology for nuclear power plants, medical devices to safely diagnose, scan, and treat the body, and a whole new inertia to more basic research and understanding. In fact, the twentieth century meant a massive boost in science and technology, both regarding knowledge creation and impact. We started that century without lightbulbs, cars, computers (nor Internet), any antibiotics nor most vaccines, planes, relativity or quantum physics, agricultural chemical fertilizers, nor knowledge of what the DNA is. This was a fantastic century for science. It is not too far-fetched to say that both World Wars were fought and won in no small part using the newly-minted scientific skills. From encryption to planes, or bombs. Life expectancy moved up in 30 years from ages 35 to 65, thanks in significant part to advances in medicine and healthcare. The "Green Revolution" of agricultural technology transfers from the '30s to the '70s boosted productivity and saved more than a billion people (granting its creator Norman Borlaug a Nobel Prize in 1970). Then, on top of all that was the Space Age. We put people on the moon, pushing engineering beyond the confines of our world, and inspiring a whole generation of kids that later pursued science and engineering.

The Moon

So profound the moon missions were, that since then, we even refer to enormous leaps of science and technology as "Moonshots." Companies, like Google, create "Moonshot Factory" divisions where the most impactful research is done. Today, when we dare to aim for almost-too-hard to achieve, we call it a Moonshot. When in 2016 the White House of the USA announced its vision to cure cancer, they called it the "Cancer Moonshot." Hard to think of a better case of what happens when a country decides to go full steam with science, technology, and research into a concrete goal. Like the Americans did with the atomic bomb. All types of scientists and engineers worked full steam ahead for a single, concrete, and very challenging goal. In the case of the moon, there were also very concrete strategic and political goals.

We went to the moon not because it was easy, nor because it was a good scientific and technological milestone. We went to the moon as part of the so-called "Space Race," a time where the Soviet Union and the USA had political and strategic pressure to show off technological progress. The Second World War was just over. The alliance to beat the Nazis was over. The Soviet Union on one side, and the USA on the other. This left two superpowers with strong political, economic, and social differences diplomatically, militarily, and socially confronted. Meanwhile, both nations were armed with increasingly more powerful nuclear weapons and long-range missiles that could destroy their respective nations. This period, called "Cold War," lasted from around 1947 to 1991, when the Soviet Union collapsed. The pressure to secretly improve their technological military capabilities, but openly signal their strength, was a strategic priority. A nation capable of launching a civilian or scientific research satellite could also use it for military uses if the need arose. The backdrop of this geopolitical struggle was a very destructive and increasingly worsened worst-case scenario. And the fuel of that progress was science and technology.

Space was the next frontier. Militarily, space could become a much quicker starting line for the new missiles; moreover, putting any technology in space meant a very high degree of technological progress. In 1955 the USA president announced plans to launch the first satellite as part of the scientific conference of the 1957 International Geophysical Year. In response, the Soviet Union decided to create a commission to beat the Americans. This was the start of the Space Race that peaked on the manned lunar landing in 1969. In general, the Soviets decided to keep secret and classified all programs, tests and launches, and only announce successes. Americans, who also had several space-grade military rocket programs, decided to create a more civilian public track—with a science, technology, and research agenda—but with clear political, military, and strategic underpinnings.

Many key scientists and engineers that helped both contenders to the Space Race were recruited Germans, some even members of the Nazi party. The so-called "Operation Paperclip" immigrated 1,600 scientists (all men). This includes Wernher von Braun, technical director of the Nazi V2 rocket (the first long-range missile). Von Braun is considered the father of rocket science in the USA and inventor of the Saturn V, the rocket that went to the moon, and that still is the most powerful rocket. In the Soviet Union, similar programs existed (like Operation Osoaviakhim, or Operation Alsos) which immigrated around 2,000 people (some at gunpoint).

The Space Race is a very complex chapter of history, but the main point here is to distill the structure and strategy to make it happen. We want to help figure out how essential science and engineering was managed so that today we refer to the Moonshot as a synonym of success. It was very clear from the beginning that there was a rush to move forward on the Space Race. At first there was no lunar goal, so the strategy was to "be first" and move the goal a bit further to be first again quickly. The first goal of the race was putting the first satellite in space, an announcement the USA made in 1955 to be in space by 1957. This "first" was Soviet on October 4th, 1957, the Sputnik, which was rushed to beat the Americans by one day, on rumors that Americans would do it on October 5th. A month later the Soviets got another first, sending the first dog, Laika. The first communication satellite, starting a whole industry, was the American Civilian Project SCORE in 1958. First civilian weather satellite, and first military image from space were the American Vanguard-2 and Explorer-6 in 1959. Also the same year, Soviets were the first lunar spacecraft and first lunar (crash) landing, the Luna-1 and Luna-2. The first human in space was the Soviet Yuri Gagarin in 1961. Likewise, Soviet was in 1961 the first robotic fly-by on Venus, Venera-1. The first woman in space was Soviet Valentina Tereshkova in 1963. The first spacewalk was also Soviet in 1965. First soft landing in the moon was Soviet, in 1966. Eventually, first humans on the moon, the American Apollo 11 in 1969. There were many more firsts, missions and whole industries started in the process of the "race to first" of the Space Race. For our impact science scope, let's look at the administration, management, and character of some of the key scientists that made it possible.

The Soviet space program was mostly classified and done directly by the military. Launches were unannounced, and only successful missions given names and publicized. Names of key people were kept secret and only released after their death. Although the Soviet Space Race started around 1955, many of the fundamentals and rocket science theory were laid by Konstantin Tsiolkovsky who died 1935.

Tsiolkovsky was a self-taught, home-schooled, hard-of-hearing, log-house dweller, reclusive genius who worked most of his life as a teacher. Some of his papers described in detail the equations and designs used decades later in space rockets, although he never built any. Both American and Soviet leading rocket engineers used may of the crucial lessons described in his papers. He also conceptualized and built prototypes of planes, dirigibles, and hovercrafts, but didn't get much attention at the time. His pioneering work started around 1880, and he retired in 1920 as a high school math teacher. Only in 1931 did he begin to receive popularized recognition, and died in 1935. Years and decades later many tributes would be made, including statues, the naming of museums or lunar craters, and even the renaming of a city in 2015.

The Soviets had several design groups competing among themselves, and with the political pressure that also sent many to prisons or Gulags (forced labor camps). For most of the Soviet Space, Sergei Korolev was the leading figure. Few colleagues knew his name and he was officially referred until his death as "Chief Designer." He was trained as a carpenter but always liked gliders and aeronautics. He did increasingly focused studies on the topic and finally graduated as an aircraft engineer in 1929, aged twenty-two. After graduation he worked on developing rockets, eventually being Chief Engineer of the main rocket research institute in the Soviet Union. He was considered very hard working, demanding, and with a strong discipline. He was a project manager who looked at every detail. In 1938, in the middle of the "Great Purge" where people considered dissenters of the Soviet Union or Lenin were prosecuted or killed, he was arrested and some of his colleagues killed. He spent a year in a gulag on a gold mine, where he sustained many injuries and lost most of his teeth. He was later moved to a sharaskha (a type of gulag where scientists are forced to do research). During this phase he developed key rocket technologies. He was released in 1944 and commissioned as a colonel in the Red Army. He flew to Germany to help bring the German scientists and engineers that, together with the Soviet ones, were placed on a fenced island under military control where their work accelerated under his good management and the absorption of the Nazi technology.

When the Space Race started in 1955 Korolev was fully rehabilitated, recognized, and a very effective science manager. It was under his command that the Soviets got most of their "firsts" we mentioned before. The actual Soviet agenda was more to advance rocket technology as weapons, and not space explorations. As the Soviets kept winning an increasingly publicized Space Race, the strategic and propaganda value of the Space Race increased, and he received more funding, resources, and pressure to keep ahead of the Americans.

He was considered the highest authority, while also an extremely demanding boss. He committed to training young graduates and to the long-term vision and impact of space. Like the Americans, he had political pressure to win the Space Race, but the experience in the gulag, and the fear of the potential consequences of losing the race kept him pushing and demanding more. These mounting pressures probably affected his health and contributed to his (not completely clarified) death in 1960, before the American flagship "first" of the manned landing on the moon.

The American Space Race was more civilian-led, more transparent, and more centralized into a stream of increasingly complex projects. After the Cold War, the US president decided to separate the civilian Space Race rockets from the military ones. They also pushed to legally establish that 100 km above ground (the "Karman line") as the end of national control, and where space begins. When Soviets launched Sputnik I and II, Americans saw on live TV the first American attempt explode on the launch pad. As Soviets gained lead with more "firsts," winning this Space Race gained political relevance and national pride, which also meant more pressure, but also more budget. It was partly this drive that led to the strategy of creating a civilian agency to direct non-military space activities, NASA. John F. Kennedy had campaigned for US president criticizing too much government spending, while promising leadership in space. He hesitated once in office by the expensive cost of NASA proposals. After the Soviets put the first man in space, the already by then American president felt the patriotic embarrassment of the Soviet lead in space. On top of that, this coincided with the defeat at the Cuban Bay of Pigs failed invasion. Kennedy asked his vice president to write up a report about their leadership in space. That report included that the USA was "neither making maximum effort nor achieving results necessary if this country is to reach a position of leadership." It also included that setting a commitment to go to the moon could recoup the loses, while being far enough that there was time to catch up to the Soviets, if given very high priority and funding. The president's scientific advisor, Jerome Wiesner, recommended against manned space exploration, and going instead with robotics. Landing robots did not carry the same patriotic value to the President, and in 1961 he went to the USA Congress to deliver his famous speech of committing to land humans on the moon and returning before the end of the decade. This commitment meant an extra budget of ~25$ billion (~220 billion adjusted for inflation), employing 400,000 staff and the support of 20,000 universities, contractors and companies. NASA, an agency born in 1958 inheriting assets and personnel from the Army and Navy among others, was to take the goal of the moon landing. The head of NASA then was James Webb, a former lieutenant and pilot from the Marine Corps. Webb hired George Muller to head the manned missions, including the Moonshot.

George Muller, born in Missouri in 1918, was the son of a stay-at-home mother and an electrician father. Muller studied electrical engineering and one of his first jobs was to help build a television transmitter. He then worked at Bell Labs, which saved him from being drafted to the military. During the war he worked on airborne radars. He realized he needed a PhD to move up the hierarchy, so he enrolled at Princeton where he took morning classes while keeping his full-time job at Bell. He got a PhD in Physics at Ohio University, and later became manager of TRW, an electronics company. While there, he started using an "all-up" testing management: test whole systems, not piece by piece. He carried this method all the way to the Apollo and the Saturn-V rocket. While in the private sector, NASA's James Webb sought him for a top job, which he only agreed to after he could substantially restructure the department. Webb appointed Muller to lead the NASA Human Space program in 1963, which halved his previous salary in the private sector. He continued pressuring the ongoing program management to get on track to win more "firsts" and lower the cost overruns. With his leadership, management style, and bold attitude, he kept pressuring the Apollo to move forward, faster. He called technical decisions, sometimes against the advice of key figures like Von Braun. When he felt he had trouble finding the right managers or skills, Muller brought up mid and junior managers from the Air Force. More than 400 military officers in total during the '60s. He was known for being an extremely good, brilliant, and fearless manager. Under his directorate, Apollo 11 landed on the moon on July 20th, 1969. He was also very involved on other famous space NASA programs beyond the Moonshot landing, like the Space Shuttle. He resigned from the administration the same year of the Moon landing, citing low salary as one of his reasons, and went back to the private sector. He died in 2015, aged ninety-seven.

From the Soviet Tsiolkovsky, Korolev, or the Americans Muller or Von Braun, we have only explored some of the key figures of the Moonshot mindset, but we can already see a pattern of tenacity despite struggles and hardship, moving forward by passion on scientific discovery, but also ruthless outcome-based management, even militaristic style and personnel. A Moonshot mindset emerges from lofty goals, clearly identified and without margins of distraction. From big budgets on political or patriotic grounds, but also relentless focus to deliver the promise. From competition, and from the interplay of academia, the private sector, politics, and military. The price of the Moonshot was high, the cost of not getting it even higher. The Moonshot stands on the shoulders of imprisoned scientists, forced labor, very tight schedules, challenging decisions, unacceptable compromises to unplanned exploration, exceptional budgets on ideological grounds, unknown heroes, exceptional milestones that succeeded but didn't count because they didn't succeed first. There is no doubt we, humankind, did the almost impossible. That achieving the moon landing pulled science and technology decades ahead than if we had not had a Space Race. It raised the baseline of human progress. But it also stretched the system so that we could achieve the goal. After the last manned Apollo landings in 1972, we have not yet returned to the moon. The average age of NASA staff during the Apollo was twenty-eight years, today it's forty-seven. The Saturn-V rocket is still unmatched, neither is the funding NASA had that lifted our science, and humans, to other planets.

Today we have a renewed interest in Space, this time coming from the private sector. We have Space X, Virgin Galactic, Blue Origin, ... Still, the same approach applies, with tightly managed science and engineering, deep pockets and a focus on relentless forward progress and achieving "firsts".

Moonshot Mindset

If we went to the moon, can we do a Cancer Moonshot and cure cancer? Can we do a Poverty Moonshot and eradicate poverty? A Climate Change Moonshot? Can we make a Moonshot Factory?

We do not have a Poverty or a Climate Change Moonshot, but we do have a Cancer Moonshot. In 2016 the US White House announced a program to find a vaccine for cancer by 2020, and they specifically called it "Cancer Moonshot." The then-president, Barack Obama, called for the "same sense of urgency and an all-hands-on-deck approach, where everybody pulled together, [...] all to look at where, if we really put our shoulder behind the wheel, where can we make the biggest impact as quickly as possible. "

In a lengthy essay, titled *Saving Science,* in the summer of 2016 issue of the *New Atlantis*, Daniel Sarewitz, professor of Science and Society at Arizona State University, argues how science is misleading itself and uses this Cancer Moonshot as an example of a way forward. The argument goes that we tend to think that science is best left alone to the curiosity of researchers, while the reality is the opposite. The idea of curiosity-driven science was put forward by Vannevar Bush, the person we introduced when we talked about the atomic bomb that was behind the American wartime science strategy, and the precursor of NASA. After the war, Bush, in his peacetime memo *Science, the endless frontier* writes: "Scientific progress on a broad front results from the free play of free intellects, working on subjects of their own choice, in the manner dictated by their curiosity for exploration of the unknown." Going to the moon, as creating the atomic bomb or other war needed innovation, was far from such curiosity-driven pursuit. It operated by military trained management, timelines, and strict procedures. The atomic bomb was run by the Department of Defense working closely with industry and researchers to pave the way. The Moonshot had partly military heritage and management. It was this attitude, and the political and superpower identity, which led us to the atomic bomb and to the moon.

The opposite, the "free play of the free intellects," Sarewitz argues, is an unaffordable luxury when it comes to achieving Moonshots. A system where science lacks an external goal or metric of progress is very hard to make accountable. If only scientists decide what to research, how to research it, and how important that is, the system feeds itself with no incentive to turn research into progress beyond keeping it alive. It is a system that promotes outputs (e.g., articles) but has no metric linking to outcomes. It is a system that eventually grows so large that would incentivize individual career building, and not collective outcomes. It is a system that, like the case we spoke on with HIV/AIDS, would favor building expertise and professional brand that secures future funding; not a system that favors outcomes, like the HIV discovery, above outputs of papers, careers, or awards.

When it comes to research on cancer, Sarewitz builds on the "sweet lie" of full academic freedom. It recounts how the US National Breast Cancer Coalition (NBCC) was born to help raise funds for academic research, eventually helping to accumulate two billion dollars in grants. At that point, at the US Congress in 2007, the NBCC president Fran Visco asks: "And what? And what is there to show? You want to do this science and what? At some point, you really have to save a life." Managing science for outcomes is very different from managing science for research. The way we teach science is a false choice between basic research or applied research, that also leaves Moonshot mindset without space. If you are in basic research, this is the domain of the "free play of the free intellect." If you are the applied research camp, your job is to take the basic research results and apply for a commercial purpose. Sarewitz is very emphatic that if Moonshots are a model for science, science should always be accountable to a mission. If a research project is exciting but is not aligned to the mission, it has no place in a Moonshot. This is the attitude for at least one of the programs inside the Cancer Moonshot, The Artemis Project, managed (in part due to funding appropriation streams) by the Department of Defense. For example, more than peer-review funding decisions, it has end-user funding decisions. Patients, advocates, and non-experts contribute in a meaningful way to the decisions of the program. This is very unorthodox academia. As the lead scientist, Dr. Dennis Slamon puts it, "[We the scientists] could not have been more wrong." The drug Herceptin, one of the most critical advances in breast cancer, was born with this management method.

This chapter cannot end without mentioning the idea of "Moonshot Factory." Is it possible to extract the process that makes a Moonshot? To make it a product, and then set it up to produce as many possible Moonshots as we can? This is exactly the hypothesis of "X," a branch of the Company Alphabet (which also owns Google). At X there are three criteria to define a possible Moonshot: first, it must aim to solve a huge problem. Second, the solution cannot be incremental, it has to be a leap of progress, at least ten times (or "10x") better. Third, this leap must start with technologies doable today. I would imagine there is a fourth criterion around the sustainability of the project itself and the approach. X is funded by its parent company Alphabet, so it is not unreasonable to think the graduating ideas ought to contribute to future revenue sources that help thrive both the for-profit corporation and the impact itself those ideas aim for. Being an impact-driven project or a for-profit project is a fall choice X embraces by design. It is very possible to create a radical solution to a huge problem that can also not only sustain itself but also bring substantial profits.

This approach of exploration without a pre-defined target or challenge to be addressed falls squarely into the "Vanebar" model of impact, where thousands of ideas are created, tried, and tested, with an unaccommodating bias away from pure curiosity detached from impact. The head of X, with a title of "Captain of Moonshots," Astro Teller refers to this phase as "failing fast," testing and trying different approaches until "eventually you fail to fail" and succeed on moving forward towards a solution. During this phase, a "Rapid Evaluation Team" works together with the team proposing a solution and they try to kill the project, to make it fail, while the other team embraces failure while looking at how to overcome the problems, how to shift focus, how to make the approach survive, and survive to the next phase of having a dedicated project building the proposed solution. X undertakes many ideas, although they are secretive to budget, staff, or even what ideas they try. They quote killing over 100 potential ideas in a year,

71

including some that had big teams, and after many months or years. Deciding to kill their own project because they discover a fundamental flaw might even be rewarded with a bonus. Such is the design for a failure culture at X. The funnel from idea to meaningful impact is huge. From millions of ideas to the next Google business that solves a problem for millions of people. A failure culture makes sure you both encourage a wide entry point in the funnel, but also that you narrow it down as soon as possible so as not to lose time or money better spent. So far, the exit point of this funnel includes a cybercrime defense company "Chronicle," an internet hot-spot service using stratospheric balloons called "Loon," a machine learning project called "Google Brain," a drone delivery service "Wing" or self-driving company "Waymo." Regarding monetary return, Waymo is valued as of 2018 at 70 billion dollars. Using "Google Brain" to optimize energy usage at Google's data centers has reportedly saved the company more than the whole cost of X since its creation.

They are not alone. Other companies embrace this model of long-term exploratory research while embracing failure and ambitious (socially and monetary) goals. In Spain, the telecommunications company Telefónica has created "Alpha." There, a team of ideation experts spend a year deciding what is the next Moonshot project, that the Board of Telefónica has to approve and commit supporting with both substantial funding and many years of runway to allow for it to succeed. Once approved, the project is publicly known and then looks for a "Moonshot Captain" that is tasked with delivery. Compared with X, Alpha resembles more the lunar Moonshot where the target is set at first, and the team has a clear direction to reach, and strong political and financial support. At X, projects are born and killed organically among the shared pool of ideas, people and funding—until the project graduates when is quite mature. In 2019, Alpha had two ongoing projects, one around personalized health services, and one around democratizing access and generation of sustainable energy.

It is tough to evaluate the success of Moonshots, their "factories," or the mindset behind them. By definition, they tend to be all or nothing, with a very high bar of success. Either the team gets to the moon or not. Either the team creates an autonomous car service or not. Either the team finds a cure for cancer or not. Moonshots involve substantial capital financially and strategically. The impact when they succeed is huge, but when they don't, they are very costly in many ways. Unlike the Lunar Moonshot, and especially with the efforts from the private sector, we have developed strategies to filter before committing, cut the costs with early ditching, let them pivot to other directions, or extract value along the way. The stakes are very high either way. To me, they highlight the fundamental tension between the explore versus exploit management in how we seek value of science in society.

Curiosity-driven science explores the unknown, with unpredictable progress in unpredictable directions. It might yield nothing new for years, or a fundamental discovery that changes everything, like Relativity. Success, in that case, is likely based on how well the wheels of the process are turning. Progress is not unexpected, but unpredictable.

Outcome-driven science, like Moonshots, not only has to progress forward to be successful, but it must also go in only one particular direction, the intended destination, and it has to get there. We probably need both. The "Moonshot Mindset" reflects on this tension by embracing impact as the selector. These Moonshot factories like X or Alpha have the luxury and responsibility of nimbly choosing their destination. That's something NASA didn't have when they went to the moon. Moreover, these Moonshots also have the luxury and responsibility to leverage tremendous resources strictly for impact. That's something academia doesn't have when publishing papers and building careers. In summary, you can't Moonshot the discovery of Relativity, but you can't get to the moon driven by academic curiosity.

Getting it Right

In previous chapters, we explored several failure cases. Instances like the HIV discovery in the USA or the case of our failure to respond as we could—and should—to climate change. We also explored the sometimes uncomfortable truths of Moonshot thinking. These are all examples where the root of the problem has strong scientific underpinnings, but as much as we can understand these, we are not able to turn this understanding into a solution, or a solution at the scale we need. While exploring these failure examples, we looked at the shortcomings and sources of this disconnect. This is a crucial part in understanding how we might have been able to do it better. To learn from these failures.

This chapter instead explores the opposite side, a few cases where we were indeed able to react, and in the same fashion, we examine the reasons why these cases were different. The "Ozone hole" crisis, in this light, is a prime example. Kofi Annan, then head of the United Nations, called it "the single most successful international agreement" during his "most comprehensive presentation of the mission of the United Nations in its 55-year history" at the Millennium Assembly of the United Nations in September 2000.

Fridges, Ozone, and Diplomats

How did something as scientifically rooted and complex as Ozone depletion chemistry, whose effect was hard to measure, poorly understood at the moment, and with strong commercial dependencies, turn out to be named by the UN as the "single most successful international agreement?" Was it the science, the way we presented it? The public understanding of the complexity? How is it different from the climate change case? Both cases, climate change and ozone depletion, are at the core a "tragedy of the commons" cases were the individual upside benefit is local, and the common downside damage is global. We emit CO2, or used CFC aerosols, because we want to use the car, or use fridges. There is a local benefit. Our actions, however, impact the global common space, everywhere, regardless if they participated in the emissions or not. Furthermore, the damage happens after some time, slowly, so it is much harder to be conscious of the global downsides than it is to be aware of the immediate local benefits.

This case study of global damage to the world starts with fridges: to cool down the food in our fridges there is a loop system that circulates gas into wider tubes inside the refrigerator and narrow ones outside. When a gas expands in the wider tubes inside the fridge, it absorbs heat, and when it contracts or condensates in the narrow outside tubes, it releases heat. That's why the back-metal grill on fridges is warmer, and the inside colder. This is similar to when heated air rises in the bathroom and it condenses on the top half of your mirror or your wall when it transfers back the heat. The key that allowed the invention of cheap fridges, in the 1920s, was the discovery of a gas that evaporates easily, so it is an efficient heat transport, but also that is not flammable, stable, easy to produce, and nontoxic.

It is worth taking a small detour to note the social context and the relation with cars. In the 1920s many house appliances were invented, like the electric iron, washing machine, radio, vacuum cleaner, the model T car, electric toaster... the USA economy was booming, and society demanded more services, more entertainment. Former luxuries became more available to more middle- or working-class people. Prominently among these, cars quickly became the anchor

79

of more freedom and new social patterns. Cars underwent continued pressures to become better, cheaper, faster, easier to use. It is in these times of change, in 1922, that a young engineer, Thomas Midgley Jr., discovered the significant improvements of adding a lead-based compound to gasoline. It made cars run smoother, with more power and efficiency.

Lead had been known to be extremely toxic since at least Greek times, but it also has very useful industrial properties: it is a ubiquitous element, and much easier to extract than its alternatives. The usefulness of this toxic substance created a complicated relationship with us. We used it in paints, in closing cans of food, soldering jewels... and now, cars. We want smoother-running cars, but we need to manage the risks. Not surprising, then, that one year after the discovery of the many benefits of leaded gasoline, shortly after receiving the 1923 Nichols Medal award, Midgley had to take an extended vacation to recover from his lead poisoning. During this decade, there is a long history of stories of leaded gasoline, the massive profits it generated due to the patents, the greater performance, and the many awards Midgley got for it. But also the continuous cases of lead poisoning, and related hallucinations, insanity, and deaths at the leaded gasoline factories. In 1924, in a press conference to demonstrate its safety, Midgley poured the gasoline additive to his hands and inhaled for sixty seconds. Soon after, he had to leave again temporarily to treat his lead poisoning. Leaded gasoline, fueled by strong industry incentives and pressures, would continue to be massively produced and demanded until the forced phasing out legislation in the '70s. Lead from the combustion gases of gasoline cars from those years can be found today worldwide, from the dust in your house to the ice in the poles.

Midgley was, by all accounts, a prolific engineer, and indeed he accumulated over 100 patents to his name over his lifetime. A few years after the leaded gasoline discovery, he turned to the problem of fridges. And he, again, made a revolutionary discovery. The product was not in itself a revolution. It was more a refinement and aggregation of the properties of known substances. The revolution was more the process to efficiently create that particular new family of compounds, the Chlorofluorocarbons (called CFCs)—and commercially called

80

"Freon." With the discovery also came very profitable patents. No known natural processes produce CFCs in significant quantities. Hence the vast majority of CFC in existence today is human-made. CFCs are, by fridge-friendly design, easy to evaporate and to absorb energy, they have low toxicity, and are non-reactive to other substances. To demonstrate its safety, in 1930, Midgley inhaled Freon and then blew a candle. Soon, Freon was used across the industry as a standard refrigerant. Furthermore, this new gas also proved very attractive for other uses such as air conditioners, aerosol sprays, asthma inhalers, fire extinguishing equipment, and many other commercials and military applications. Indeed, Midgley won the Perkin Medal in 1937 for this work. Soon after, in 1941, he also won the Priestley Medal, the Willard Gibbs Award in 1942, and in 1944 was elected to the US National Academies of Sciences, and President of the American Chemical Society.

Unbeknownst to the world, the essential design properties of CFCs proved the most harmful. Being so stable, CFCs mix in the air and remain stable for many decades. As they mix in the air, when they reach the upper atmosphere, the more energetic ultraviolet light of the Sun can finally break it down. Ultraviolet light is absorbed up there by oxygen-producing ozone, hence removing this solar radiation in the lower parts of the atmosphere. When CFCs reaches the same regions where the ozone is, it also gets broken apart. The CFC pieces, unlike the whole molecule, are very reactive, and their mere presence makes ozone break apart, disabling their blocking effect, which in turn produces more reactions. It is now understood that a single CFC molecule released on the ground takes roughly seven years to reach the upper atmosphere and can stay there for a century, catalyzing the destruction of 100,000 ozone molecules. This weakening of ozone protection happens everywhere in the upper atmosphere, but much more so with the presence of extremely cold clouds, like the ones in the poles during spring, when these clouds interact with the solar light. Hence the Ozone hole happens more in the poles. At its worst moment, the Antarctic Ozone layer lost 70% of its protecting strength. With less ozone to protect us, more ultraviolet radiation reaches the ground, which can produce sunburns, cataracts and several types of cancers in

81

humans. It also affects phytoplankton and marine animals, and even crops as ultraviolet radiation, for example, can kill the bacteria upon which some plants, such as rice, depend on to grow. Moreover, CFCs are also potent greenhouse gases that trap heat in the lower atmosphere, contributing to climate change that in turn, when trapping heat in the lower atmosphere, reduce the temperature in the upper parts, contributing to more active CFC ozone depletion.

Although this chapter is about the success of the response to this global threat, it was worth to note how much a single person, the engineer Midgley, contributed to useful advances to society, but also extreme damage to the atmosphere. As J.R. McNeill, an environmental historian, puts it, he had "more impact on the atmosphere than any other single organism in Earth's history." Several of his key creations proved fatal in the end. Ironically, as Bill Bryson tells in the book *Short History of Nearly Everything*, Midgley died from his resourcefulness. In 1940, he contracted polio, a disease that left his legs paralyzed for life. In his inventiveness, he devised a pulley system to assist himself in bed, and in 1944, aged fifty-five and before he knew about the problems with the ozone, he got entangled on his device and died strangling himself.

It wasn't until 1973 when research scientists started to understand, and worry, about the effects of CFC once they reach the upper atmosphere. The hypothesis of CFC weakening the ozone layer was still unproven. The chemistry of CFC-Ozone is very complex and took many more years to understand it, especially its effects on polar clouds. The dangers of more ultraviolet light were, however, more understood. Hence, if true, an increase of radiation-induced cancer and other problems were a logical consequence of increased CFCs. Meanwhile, usage of these gases had increased dramatically for its many benefits and applications, proving to also be very profitable to the patent holders, namely the company DuPont. Like in the case of HIV appearance, the industry pressures were strong. Millions of people used daily CFC-dependent products, from fire extinguishers to aerosol sprays or refrigeration devices. Moreover, there were no comparable alternatives. The chairman of DuPont, in 1975, called the CFC-Ozone hypothesis "a science fiction tale... a load of rubbish... utter nonsense," and so complained many other industrial users of CFCs.

Unlike the HIV case, the same year that the first scientific findings pointing to an impending crisis were published, in 1973, the authors were asked to testify before US Congress, after which funding became available to explore the issue of ozone depletion and CFCs. This was a very positive response, probably among the key early precursors of the positive outcome. It is hence worth exploring a bit further how this came to be. At first glance, it would be accurate, and true, to claim that a key difference is that AIDS only affected a minority group that also was ostracized (gay community). While this can be the case, and draws a valuable lesson to understand the differences, we will see that other factors compounded to the positive response to the ozone crisis.

It is very possible that supersonic commercial flights played a key role. In the '60s in the USA, a heavily federally subsidized program was put in place to create supersonic commercial flights. A similar project was started in Europe by French and British governments (what later became the Concorde). Besides the political and economic struggles of the program, the environmental impact had many worrying fronts: from sonic booms, or engine noise to the poisonous exhaust gases of the new fuel that was needed. Thus, in 1971, the US Congress commissioned a scientific comprehensive study of the climate impact of these supersonic flights. It involved 500 scientists and two years. When the report came out in December 1974, the executive summary, meant for the public, ignored several of the key scientific concerns raised on the report itself (over 9,000 pages). The report included evidence linking weakening of the stratospheric natural filters of solar radiation with cancer. When this scientific report, and the controversy of its misleading summary, came out, there was a growing environmental movement and an increased awareness of environmental problems due to human activities. It was also in 1974 that the young researcher Mario Molina and his supervisor published an article in *Nature* with a proposed mechanism of how the CFC might destroy the ozone (he later won the 1995 Nobel Prize for this discovery). At the time, January 1975, the parallel issue of CFCs on spray cans took enough prominence to grant another independent study by the National Science Foundation. It was aptly named "Interagency Task Force on Inadvertent

83

Modification of the Stratosphere" and was joined by another study by the National Academies of Sciences. This growing tradition of creating merged commissions of scientists, policymakers and media prepared the foundations for the CFCs-ban success. By 1976 the US (and Canada, Sweden, Denmark, and Norway) upon learning of these recent studies on the impacts of CFC, officially started considering regulations for aerosol spray cans.

The Reagan administration in the USA proved resistant to regulations in response to this growing set of environmental studies. This was in part based on the tentative nature of the scientific findings, and especially after the National Academies studies downgraded the initial estimates of impact from their original report. Moreover, the patented CFCs—Freon—had a rapidly growing set of applications, for which the demand and market was also growing. These growing commercial markets created strong private sector incentives against more regulations, which ultimately was also affecting consumers, who demanded more of those products and didn´t want to see higher prices due to more regulations or special taxes. Finally, in 1978 the US banned CFC-based aerosol sprays, a move that did not happen in Europe, or for other CFC applications. As time moved on, in parallel with growing evidence of the environmental impact, the private sector incentives began to change as the critical Freon patent which protected DuPont´s market position, was about to expire in 1979, while the demand for this gas temporarily diminished with the aerosol ban. The private sector incentive of product development, for which the concept of "patent protection" was invented, had then increasing incentive to make a new product. Foreshadowing what could happen in the following years, it became strategical to develop a new product, hence a new patent. If that product proved less harmful, it would also have the backing of the environmentalists and the public sector to pivot the market under the new patent, just as the old one expired.

In 1983, William Ruckelshaus was appointed, again, as the new head of the US Environmental Protection Agency (EPA). Ruckelshaus, from Indianapolis (Indiana, USA), was a Republican attorney with no formal training in science. Instead, right after high school, he served in the army and later studied history at Princeton and law at Harvard. He then worked as an Indiana State Attorney General and was appointed to the Indiana Board of Health. This mix of knowledge of law and health were probably beneficial when he was asked, in 1970, to create and head the EPA. Shortly after its creation the agency banned the use of the very effective but poisonous pesticide "DDT," overruling the decision of a judge that found it not to be a confirmed hazard, setting a strong precedent of public safety over industrial interest. In 1973, following the Watergate scandal, Ruckelshaus left the EPA to be Acting Director of the FBI and shortly after went to the private sector. Back at the EPA in 1983, the Ruckelshaus EPA that had banned DDT pushed for CFC regulations to move forward.

In 1985 new measurements of ozone depletion, or weakening, were reported near the South Pole, and it was speculated to be related to CFCs. In the media, for this first time, this was widely echoed and reported as the NASA discovery of the "Antarctic Ozone Hole." This happened in parallel with several scientific and policy-making workshops that helped globalize the new research science into regulatory pressures globally for all potentially signatory countries. Those countries which had banned spray cans were keen to push for regulations, while several European nations favored weaker reductions due to economic and political reasons.

In 1986, the EPA published a study estimating 150 million skin cancer diagnoses and more than 3 million deaths in the U.S. population born before 2075. Meanwhile, a series of expeditions to Antarctica confirmed the ozone hole due to human-made CFCs. With this clearer linkage to cancer, and the fact that few companies were the patent holders (and now potentially liable), the industry began to support regulation and production bans, while more countries joined. In 1985 it was agreed to phase out completely all CFCs by 2000 (2010 in less developed countries). That year, twenty nations and most of the major CFC producers signed the Vienna convention, establishing a framework to negotiate an international regulation on Ozone-affecting substances. With the renewed media attention, eighteen months later in 1987 in Montreal, that agreement was signed. That agreement pledged to freeze production growth and reduce production by 50% by 1999.

This is not to say that all stakeholders quickly changed their minds. Indeed, in 1987, DuPont, at the time the primary producer of CFC, testified in Congress they believed "there is no imminent crisis that demands unilateral regulation." The lack of good alternatives, and profitable patents from a few powerful industry players, like DuPont, was a constant struggle to replace CFCs with less harmful gases. Parallel to the commercial incentives of these few companies, in 1992, the patent of a new ozone-safe alternative developed by a German technological institute was given to Greenpeace. Greenpeace quickly made this new option, named "Greenfreeze," open source and started to work with manufacturers to promote it as a replacement of CFCs. Helped by CFC bans rolling out in several countries, usage of Greenfreeze reached 40% of the market worldwide by 2013. In the USA, industry-backed lobbyists managed to delay approval of Greenfreeze usage until 2011.

Since 1987, and the first approval of the agreement in Montreal, this commitment has been reinforced substantially several times in response to more scientific evidence, pressure from NGOs and media reporting. More ozone-depleting substances were added, more countries signed, and more finance mechanisms were given to less developed countries to assist their efforts to phase out controlled substances. The ban on producing CFCs and other ozone-depleting substances came into effect in 1989, the ozone level ceased to get worse in the mid-90s, and began to recover in the 2000s. It is expected to reach pre-CFC levels by 2075, roughly a century after its creation.

To summarize, in 1973 we had the first, partial, and tentative scientific evidence. The evidence grew in parallel to the work of committees mixing scientist, lawmakers, and media, and the shifting commercial incentives and global politics. At first, in the '70s, several countries, some being primary producers of CFC, began regulating or banning CFC aerosols domestically. While these proved effective in limiting national emissions, it also made clear that the CFC was a global issue that needed a global framework. Then, building on these efforts under the UN Environmental Program, a comprehensive multi-national approach emerged which yielded the 1987 Montreal conference. That year, eleven countries representing two-thirds of all

CFCs consumed signed the deal, even before environmental or human impacts were conclusively detected. Since then, we have had both more scientific evidence and, in parallel, reinforced and expanded provisions of the Montreal Protocol, new patent-free green alternatives, and a more demanding public awareness of the link between cancer and CFCs. Today, most ozone-depleting gases are regulated and their emissions eliminated or controlled. It is worth noting that this work is far from complete. Old appliances and in storage still use CFCs, as well as some limited authorized uses for safety and critical assets where alternatives don't work. Moreover, recent research[19] has found that a specific type of CFC is still being emitted somewhere, probably around Asia. It is hard to know if these are from old storage units or actively being produced against the regulations. This emphasizes the critical role of monitoring and continued research to further understand the dangers, quickly identify violations of the treaties, and act upon them. The *tragedy of the commons* becomes a collaborative effort to protect the commons.

The first scientific evidence of ozone depletion due to CFCs came with very concrete and scary consequences: skin cancer. These were not complete scientific understandings, and indeed it took many years to gain enough knowledge to model the consequences or the impact of policy decisions properly. In parallel, society, via consumer demands, was also eager and hungry for the products that use the very same compounds that they identified with more cancer through the media. The increasing demand and profits increased in parallel, reinforcing the resistance to act. Hence, the Montreal Protocol not only agreed on the reasons to regulate CFCs but also incorporated, from the start, mechanisms to modify, control and adapt the economy to the increasing scientific evidence. It provided incentives and mechanisms both for government and private sector entities, such as trading mechanisms of existing reserves, differential due dates depending on the economic development of different countries or public funds to support the removal of CFC reserves. Moreover, only signatory countries could trade CFC among themselves. Once the main producers signed up, the rest had to follow suit as they were very dependent on the trading. Differential due dates for different countries implementing

CFC reductions proved key as well. Developing countries were given longer phase-out pathways and funding mechanisms. The list of controlled substances and industries was explicit and articulated, giving clear prioritization and equal transparency to all stakeholders involved to get moving. Lastly, and quite importantly, by the time the agreement was signed, several key patents were due to expire, which provided further incentive for the private sector to phase out the old CFC into something new. With a clear global and reinforcing agreement, research on new products, and patents, had a visible design scope and a predictable and profitable global market eager to adopt the new products with safer, greened, and under the Montreal Protocol, like Greenfreeze.

The Montreal Protocol in this sense proved much more effective than the Kyoto Protocol on climate change. The Kyoto Protocol is about reducing CO_2 mostly by trading emission rights. Every country was given a set diminishing quota, and those emitting more would need to pay to those emitting less for their rights to emit. Those countries that are emitting less tend also to be less developed nations, which also suffer more of the consequences of climate change. Thus, in effect, this protocol imposes an incentive to emit less for polluting countries, and provides finance for those needing it the most, an incentive so they can develop directly into less emitting societies. While the effectiveness of the Kyoto Protocol is debated, especially against the backdrop of not having any CO_2-reduction fully-enforced agreement, it is clear that the Montreal Protocol was able to achieve key results that Kyoto was not. For example, neither US, China, India, or Russia have binding targets, are not signatory members, or failed to ratify their commitments. As outcomes goes, CO_2 continues to rise, while CFC levels are unequivocally reduced as results of the Montreal Protocol.[20]

Saving Babies with Hot Wax

Not all success stories of impact science in this book involve multi-national global agreements over decades, like the cases in previous pages on climate change or the ozone layer. The following successful example is more on the power an individual can have. Thus, in a more personal sense, very inspiring. This is the story of Jane Chen and her company "Embrace."

In 2007, Jane was attending a new course at her MBA in Stanford titled "Entrepreneurial Design for Extreme Affordability." The course aims to design solutions to problems that otherwise have very expensive solutions. Jane and her group chose to tackle neonatal mortality. The most common cause of death of infants is preterm birth (defined as babies born prematurely before their 37 weeks after conception). There are around 15 million preterm births globally every year. In the developed world, the survival rate is 90%, while in the developing world it is the staggering opposite, 10% survival rate. It is estimated that up to 75% of these babies could survive if supplied constant warmth, breastfeeding, and protection from infections. In fact, in developed countries, the most common treatment is to put the preterm baby in an incubator with a temperature regulator to keep the baby at constant warmth. These are profoundly sad numbers that reflect a very harsh reality that is essentially exclusive to underdeveloped conditions. In fact, one of the signs of development is how quickly neonatal and child mortality improves as countries evolve and can afford better health facilities, as people—especially women—receive better education and as governments can provide better public services[21]. In essence, what Jane set up to do is to break the dependency of infant survivability and poverty. To try to find a very cheap and easy way to dramatically reduce the preventable deaths of millions of babies across the world. No small task.

One of the critical parts of this problem is that incubators are expensive, difficult to handle, need training to use them, they need constant electricity, and also maintenance servicing. Yet, incubators are precisely one of the key resources the developed world uses to save lives of preterm babies. Unfortunately, these devices are luxuries in themselves and the resources they need to work correctly in many parts of the world, as Jane found on her first fact-finding trip to India. They saw rooms with many babies in need of care. If there were incubators, they were sometimes empty, in the corner of the room, turned off, unused. Maybe there is no electricity, or there is a broken piece they can't replace, or they just haven't received the proper training to use it. While preparing for this book, this was exactly my experience when I visited the hospital at Kakuma refugee camp, in Kenya, with 180,000 refugees. The main health facility had two incubators and both were unused already for many months, due to some spare part that was missing. Around the world where incubators are missing or unusable, health facilities resort to use blankets or, when there is electricity, light bulbs for warmth, which is dangerous and very inefficient. Keeping the baby with a constant warm temperature easily and cheaply is much harder than it might appear at first.

In parallel to this life or death challenge, every person who has gone to high school and done basic physics, harbors in their mind the key scientific concept at the core of what Jane and her team built. It is incredibly frustrating to realize, in retrospect, that one has, at the same time, knowledge of such a profound challenge, and knowledge of a solution for it. That's how I felt when I met Jane a few years ago when I had just told her about this whole idea of impact science. Hopefully, by delaying writing here what that key concept is, I am conveying this very point. There is a key fundamental physical property that all of us know, and that can save the lives of millions of babies. Part of the reason I believe scientists should have a place on the table in seemingly unconnected topics is precisely cases like this one. Although in this case this is a basic one, the tools and factoids of a trained scientist could be applied in very unexpected places.

The foundation of Jane's solution is knowing that water freezes below 0 degrees Centigrade (32 Fahrenheit). You cannot have water below that freezing temperature, as it becomes ice. In fact, if you place water under very cold conditions, the water will freeze faster. Besides experiencing this many times in our own lives, in high school you might have learned the name of this process, "phase transition." From liquid to solid, in this case. One of the core observations is that during a transition of phase, the temperature stays constant. The speed of change might differ, but the temperature remains constant throughout the process. Any substance will release energy—temperature—if the surroundings are colder and absorb energy than if the surroundings are hotter. The temperature will change at various speeds, but if the change in temperature crosses a change of phase (like 0C/32F for water) the substance will stay at that temperature until all of it has changed phase. In other words, when it's hot, ice melts; and if it's very hot, ice melts quickly. When it's cold water freezes; when it's very cold, water freezes quickly. Moreover, it takes much more energy to cross a phase transition than it takes to change the temperature when it doesn't involve one.

Taking this realization to neonatal mortality, the problem becomes finding a substance that melts/solidifies at the temperature the baby needs. That way physics will ensure a constant temperature. That substance turns out to be a combination of different waxes, although Jane tells the story that they first tried a prototype with butter, making a huge mess of melted butter, plastics, and cloth in the process.

Simplifying it, you heat up a sealed plastic pocket with wax inside in boiling water. Once warm, the plastic holds a warm liquid wax. You put a cloth cover over the pocket of wax that shapes the product as a sleeping bag for the baby. The wax will release constant temperature for a few hours as it cools down to room temperature, and changing phase into solid. After a few hours, when the wax is harder, you can then heat it up again. Compared to the cost of an incubator, this is several orders of magnitude cheaper, and much easier to manufacture, operate, and maintain. The wax is cheap material, as they also are the plastic pockets, the sleeping bag cover, and the process to boil the wax pocket in water.

The conceptual breakthrough here, the science fact, is done, but of course this is only a small piece of the solution that later became the company "Embrace". In the process, Jane and the team had to face many challenges—from finding a sustainable business model to adjusting to cultural differences. The success of the product—both regarding doing all the product development and later manufacturing and distribution—but success also in regards to saving lives, depends on many factors, like any other startup. Some of these challenges could have stronger scientific underpinnings, like the physics of phase transition, and some less so, like figuring out philanthropic or for-profits models that would maximize the impact. Among these challenges, for the context of this book, it's also worth mentioning the cultural aspects of western numeric accuracy and protocols. As Jane explains on her experience with the first version of the product, it turns out that in India there is a perception of western medicine to be too strong, so there is a tendency to adapt it by weakening it. For example, giving smaller doses of a medicine or shortening the treatment. In the case of Embrace, the wax pockets had temperature indicators with numbers to make sure the temperature was neither too high—hence dangerous—or too cold—and ineffective. This can happen if the pocket is heated too much and the wax is well above the transition phase temperature, so it needs to cool down until the transition phase starts and the temperature becomes constant. If the wax is too cool not all the material has changed phase and it will last too short, or not even get to the right temperature if all the wax is solid. The problem was that caregivers would not heat the pockets properly as they would adjust what they thought was a better temperature number than prescribed. The solution the team found was to replace the numerical indicator of degrees, with a simpler three symbols indicator: too cold, okay temperature, too hot. This was a simple adjustment but a key one, result of a development process iterating quickly as the first users started to use the product. In this case, more data, more "scientific" information was detrimental to the outcome.

The project started as a class assignment, which turned into two years living in India setting up the non-profit and starting to provide the services. The enterprise lived from donations and partners from Gates Foundation, Beyoncé or Mark Benioff, and the awards and praise of the then USA President Obama, the Skoll foundation, the Schwab Social Entrepreneurs of the Year, or Forbes' Impact 30. The project has since developed a dual operation where one side donates the product to places in most need and without resources, and the other side sells them to governments and private partners that can afford it, at a price that also covers the cost of the donations. In 2016 the company reported having helped more than 200,000 babies across twenty countries.

When you read the story or watch her online videos[22] it's clear that Embrace is a huge achievement, and that the wax transition phase trick, while being a core scientific key principle, it's also a tiny part to make it successful. When I met Jane and learned her story, I did, however, wonder what other lifesaving product and services rest upon other basic, or not basic, scientific principles I might already know. I wonder what would happen if we tell more stories like this one, if we motivate more people to connect the dots between a real problem and seemingly unrelated scientific fact or model.

It is also tempting to frame this achievement as the advantage of an "interdisciplinary research." Innovation usually happens at the interface of different expertise. There is indeed a recent, and needed, push towards removing silos and collaborations researching across domains. The transition of wax phase and neonatal mortality is clearly an enormous success story of connecting domains, but at the same time it seems extremely unlikely at first. No physicist or chemist would answer "neonatal mortality" to the question of why we should research wax, unless they knew about the problem. No public health development expert would find "melting wax" as a potential solution to neonatal mortality unless they realized the link beforehand. One design solution is to maximize interface crossing, creating multidisciplinary teams. But, with how many fields of expertise, how many permutations of how many experts, and with which kinds of networking events would it take to make wax and neonatal mortality a likely match?

Moreover, I worry about the disconnect between the realization of the potential and the actual product. This is a much general entrepreneurship message, but at the same time I firmly believe the process could be eased having an impact scientist that could move back and forth between and across scientific knowledge silos, and pragmatic applications.

An impact scientist is not someone who learns about the connection, neither one that publishes the potential on an academic paper (which can very well do), but someone who helps in the whole process from idea to product, trying to help each step of the way. In the process of writing this book I've seen that pipeline, or funnel, in a few cases. First, comes the *curious* person who discovers the potential (in this case, phase transition could help solve neonatal mortality). Second comes the *academic/engineer* who puts forward the hypothesis and figures out in more detail how this could (in this case, which waxes, and how the whole thing works). Third comes the *impactor* who builds the first prototypes, business model, and setup to go for the rest of the way to impact.

Here is another case. Someone plays with image compression and computer file formats and realizes some details of the image get consistently lost or degraded after compression. You realize you can build a program to compare and learn what or how details get lost, what artifacts are created, and how they differ, with different image compressions. A *curious* person realizes that you can also, given a compressed image with artifacts, train a computer to extrapolate back a possible original image. You can make computers in essence "hallucinate." The reconstruction will be fake, but likely to be roughly correct (humans do it, a pink-haired person far away looks like a person with a pink hat). This would make a good academic article, and in fact such papers have been written. Now, the *impactor* also realizes there is a huge application in cases where the exact detailed image is not that important as it is to compress the image a lot (bad internet connections, online games with many players at once …). And so, the impactor builds a solution. That solution, and this story, happens to be a real company called "Magic Pony" that was funded in 2014 and acquired for 150 million dollars in 2016[23].

Walking the Path, Blind

When looking at this model of impact science, going from the *curious* profile pushing knowledge generation, to the *impact* profile pulling from the solution mindset, I look for failure cases and I look for success cases. I think we can learn from both. And I also look for cases in the middle, either because it shows signs of both, or because it's still evolving. A prime case of that is Mark Pollock's case, and the Druid Collective.

Mark is a tough northern Irish, if I may use a redundancy. Due to a health condition, he became blind in 1998 and after suffering depression, he used adventure and overcoming physical endurance challenges as a way to build up again his identity and character. He ended up running marathons in the desert or racing to reach the North Pole. Blind. He also then found his love and life companion, Simone George. Life and its turns had it that he would soon have to apply his own motivational speeches overcoming hardship and handicaps. He suffered an accident in 2010 and became paralyzed from the waist down. Blind and paralyzed. I can't fathom how one comes back from that, but they did, and Mark and Simone are fully dedicated to combine robotics, sensors and electrical stimulation so he can walk again. When I met him in 2013 I was deeply moved, impressed, and also skeptical of him finding a way to make paralyzed people walk again. So many factual reasons to doubt. This is where the story hits impact science. Neither of them are trained scientists, but they know the solution to their challenge will have a lot of science. A lot of academic knowledge, but also a lot of experimentation, a lot of new potential paths, a lot of combining fields of research, technology, and personal grit to endure the challenge.

Fast forward to 2018 and Mark has found that there are companies that build smart exoskeletons, like "Ekso Bionics." You strap them on and their sensors and motors can do all the walking. He has walked over one million steps. Turns out physically moving as if you walk is important not only for the muscles but also the severed nervous system. In parallel, they found academic research on noninvasive electrical stimulations. Basically, small electric shocks on the skin above the muscle triggers muscle contraction and, in some cases, can slowly help regain some sensation, internal functions and hopefully some degree of mobility. What Mark and Simone did, was to combine all these pieces with a stubborn focus on impact: to walk again. They partnered with UCLA researchers, with bionic experts, data experts, and anyone who could help them figuratively and literally walk the path of regaining mobility. As of 2019, combining all these techniques, the smart exoskeleton does not need to do all the work, the electrical stimulations have allowed him to trigger voluntary movement. The path of recovery, while far from clear of obstacles, has already shown both progress and directions beyond what has ever been done before.

One of the key difficulties is that these kinds of applications demand very deep knowledge of several scientific and technical fields, such as robotics and electrical stimulations, they succeed with complex networks of incentives, the right type of investors, and a wider but solid bridge between technology, market, and sustainable business models. These kind of companies are sometimes called "deep tech," and while their upside might open whole markets, they are harder to run, need a lot of upfront capital, find investors, iterate with users... this is exactly the space, and with Mark Pollock's case as canonical example, that the "Druid Collective" was set up to help[24]. To help identify these companies, to find and offer technical help, match with the right investors, the right partners, or help identify the best and shortest paths to market. The Druid Collective includes investors, former ministers, impact scientists, and end-users of these efforts like Mark Pollock or Simone.

Science or tech innovation around health care or health conditions are a very special case of impact science. Especially for patients of an "incurable" condition. Even the name *patient* gives an idea of the frustration of being relegated to be passive and wait for research to find a cure or a treatment. Mark, Simone, and a growing number of rare disease patients and their families are shifting the status quo. Their interest is not necessarily to understand how and why symptoms happen, or the cause of it, as it is a means to find solutions, either cures or treatments to handle the consequences or handicaps, to have a better lifestyle. There is a long shadow of doubt that one might cross the line and give false hopes of finding a cure to save their life, but there is clearly a huge space where patients becomes active stakeholders of the challenge. Mark and Simone represent a huge example of this, but there are many other initiatives, like "Patients Like Me" or "Rare Connect"[25] where people with health conditions upload their data—from daily mood to prescription or physical activity—so they can both enable traditional research, but also explore other options or conversation among families with similar conditions.

In all these cases, from the hot wax incubator, to regaining personal mobility, there are strong scientific and technological underpinnings. I read them, and I reflect on this pipeline model of impact science. I realize that my training is academic in the sense that I feel most prepared, and interested, in the part about making and validating hypothesis, creating knowledge. I also see that the most impact happens when going the whole way. It is fair to think that these are distinct roles to be done with different people, but I would contend that the funnel between scientific discoveries and making a difference in the world could widen substantially if we bring the scientists closer to the impact. Especially as the world becomes increasingly dominated by scientific and technological products, services, and data. As this progress creates ever more complexity, it is very important that more people are engaged not only with their use, but also the tools to create them, to democratize the tools and process of progress, not only the products of progress. Reframing the role of scientist into impact helps expand the focus of what a scientist is or does, away from only knowledge creation and into more generally the power of the scientific tools, especially when combined alongside other stakeholders, experts, and users.

Teaching how to Change the World

Virtually all scientists come from academic institutions, such as universities. However, most universities only train research scientists, with little space for non-research career paths, this is especially the case for "pure sciences" like physics, biology, chemistry, or math. Usually there are a few sessions about other careers, programs to transfer into, other degrees such as journalism or teaching, but usually this is the exception rather than a possible option. Most scientists we can identify today as impact scientists, are more the result of a path that started in universities, perhaps includes some graduate or postgraduate experience, but then felt their path was not leading in the right direction of impact, so they had to steer off into the unknown. It often includes a phase of uncertainty or reconversion, and definitely was not something recommended when studying. Thankfully, this is changing. This change was probably helped both by the "Data Science" revolution, but also the millennial generation, known for being particularly minded about social impact[26], getting to university age. This section explores some of these efforts from the educational space to create the profile of a scientist much closer to impact, not only focused on research or academia.

One of the most prominent examples of educational efforts is precisely the class where Jane Chane started working on the Embrace company we wrote about in the last chapter. At Stanford, the university where it happens, it is called the "D School," or "Hasso Plattner Institute of Design at Stanford University." Besides fostering the creation of Jane's solution Embrace, they are also known for the creation of "d.light," a company that creates a very low-cost solar-powered artificial lights. This company started in 2006, the year before Jane took the class. By 2017 they had "sold close to twenty million solar light and power products in 62 countries, improving the lives of over 82 million people," according to their website.

"D School" has become a hugely demanded class at Stanford. Increasingly globally-minded students, also knowledgeable in complex science and technology skills, look to make a difference in the world. They are aware of the potential they might be able to have, but feel unable to connect their skills with these multi-dimensional complex challenges. The process in this class, as described by David Kelly in a 2013 New York Times profile[27], is first to boost their "creative confidence" so that they are aware of this potential. They then learn "ideation processes," where rapid prototyping and user feedback become key strategies to incorporate their scientific and technical skills into this creative confidence.

Another place catering to this impact science demand is a class called "How to change the world" at the University College in London´s Department of Science, Technology, Engineering, and Public Policy. This class occurs once a year and lasts for two weeks. In 2017, when I met its director, Dr. Jason Blackstock, it attracted 700 students across the sciences to include engineering, chemistry, computer science. They are all met by 65 experts from the public and private sector, and presented with global challenges, such as safe water drinking in refugee camps, or reducing carbon dependence in everyday products[28]. The first week is structured to push them from the overall context of the challenge towards a concrete part they are uniquely positioned to make an impact, gathering in groups with different skills; which might include partnering with external experts. The design of this class favors groups with a wide range of skills and experiences, and with a clear goal. In the end, not only do they experience the process of realizing the value of the scientific and technical skills, but also how hard it is to integrate this into the complex reality of global challenges, with their political, cultural, or strategic dimensions. The underlying strategy of the university is to foster impact by easing the links and partnership building skills of students between academia, policy-making, and industry.

As hinted by the example of these two schools, every year there is more attention to widen the mindset of how science influences society. Obviously via academia and research, but there is much more space to drive positive impact in the world with scientists. One way of looking the difference between academia or research, and impact science is to see the focus of these new schools on "pulling" from the specific impact they seek to have, rather than "pushing" academically trained scientists or academic knowledge into impact. One of the key differences is that when you push, you need to know more or less which direction and what knowledge you are going to be pushing. When you pull, the goal is much clearer by definition, and it is much easier to explore and guide what is it you need to consider or incorporate to get the solution. You could push, for example, the knowledge of new lithium batteries into climate change, and we should. You can also think of energy use and seek how pull solutions, either being new batteries, consumption incentives, or work with biggest consumers. We tend to think of, and train for, scientists and their skills in the first case, but not so much for the second case, even when their skills are equally applicable.

Moreover, this is not just about getting scientists to explore other domains, to reach out into problems whose knowledge domain seems far away, or to incentive interdisciplinary scientists. There are far too many combinations of disciplines in science to cover all combinations that might get to a particular solution. This is still a "push" mindset. This is about radically flip the equation, from knowledge-based value, to skills-based value. To create a work space when, given a concrete set of very pragmatic and convoluted problems, we can cluster experts and stakeholders together, and then combine in equal terms the inputs from each one, including impact scientists, so we can get to a solution. This is exactly what can explain the creation, and explosive growth of "Data Science," as we pointed out in the Introduction section of this book. Data scientists pull from the questions they need to answer. They use formal mathematics, models, hypothesis—but all with the mindset of pulling this work into an answer. In fact, one of the biggest risks for a data scientist, or working with big data, is not having a concrete question and spending too much time looking for interesting questions one might solve with the data. While this is great for academic curiosity, the incentive of the private sector is probably in supporting decision making, not supporting curiosity. This mindset on skill-based value is so dominant, that there is a boom in schools of data science where they directly teach these formerly academic skills. While most of these cater the specifics of tech companies and start-ups, there is a wide range of those who seek wider impact with data science. To name two examples: "Fast.ai" and "Data

Science for Social Good". "Fast.ai" is a company dedicated to teaching machine learning so that is understood by as many people as possible, with a special emphasis on social problems and diversity. It is led by Rachel Thomas, a PhD in mathematics turned data scientist, and Jeremy Howard a self-thought machine learning expert and data scientist. The second example, "Data Science for Social Good," is a course at the University of Chicago which also teaches data science, but specifically for its application on social problems, with a strong emphasis on working with real projects with partnerships with NGOs, local governments, or international institutions such as the World Bank. This project is led by Rayid Ganhi, a former data scientist of the Obama campaign who saw the power of data science skills and decided to work with scientists to focus this potential into positive social impact.

How do we get there, Handbook for Scientists and Managers

In this book I argue that science is not just about papers, or even understanding—science is about gathering understanding *in order to* improve as humans, as societies. We have been increasingly obsessed with the *what*, or the *why* of things, but not the *so what*. This book argues, using stories and examples rather than theory, about this forgotten space of science in a world increasingly dominated and driven by data and technology.

This book is aimed at anyone who seeks not only answers, but real impact from science. Anyone who is curious about the world, but also seeks to connect this curiosity with the complicated distance between understanding and the real word. We have covered stories of poverty reduction, fighting the ozone hole or curing scurvy.

This book is also directed to scientists who want to round up their skills to be more effective outside of academia or research. It argues for creating a bigger supply of impact scientists. Lastly (and perhaps more importantly), it also argues for creating a bigger demand for those impact scientists.

This book is therefore aimed also for business executives, managers, and hiring professionals in the private sector, as well as public officials, chiefs of staff, and politicians who struggle with hiring and managing scientists for fear they are stuck exclusively in research, or have a harder time aligning their scientific skills for the mandate of the company—or the messy reality of governance and making public policy.

In order to be as useful as possible this last section of the book is a distilled handbook of recommendations advice on creating or managing impact scientists.

This chapter builds in a good part on my own experience and motivations, but it also includes the external perspectives from each of my bosses and managers since I left academia. I traveled to sit down with each of my bosses years after we worked together: at my last academic postdoc, the CEOs of the NGOs and the startups I worked at, and my World Bank manager. I wanted to understand what they saw different in my profile or attitude. If this is a typical transition from academia to impact science, I'm trying to understand how I was different, and what was good and what was bad at each step. To accumulate more than my anecdotal evidence, I have also travelled the world for two years to more than twenty countries testing my hypothesis of impact science as a consultant, and to interview academics, employees, managers, investors, and politicians that are, or work with, academics that have left academia, or wanted to. It also draws from the feedback of talks, consulting and events I've done, including a session back at my PhD institution; and mentees I have helped throughout these years. Lastly, I have been very deliberate in seeking continuous feedback on this book from the earliest drafts. I have registered and integrated all of this feedback and continue to do so through its website (impactscience.dev/). Feedback from readers is always welcome. In fact, this book is meant to be updated regularly, so make sure to check online for the latest version.

Managing Science for Impact

Recently, an investor friend asked for my feedback and help. It was with one of his healthcare companies, one that was mostly based on the commercial application of a research discovery. I can't share the details, but the goal was a profound advance in the treatment of a major type of deathly disease. Getting an effective treatment would be a hard process, as it involved some behavioral changes, but the upside had a huge potential benefit. A medical Moonshot. The main engineer, a published researcher that was making his name on this project, was the linchpin of the company, but it was impossible to manage. No commitment to timelines, no real justification of budget needs, incomplete documentation, unable to externalize tasks to move faster, and endless research side projects were some of my friend's concerns. I felt somewhat identified with that scientist. He shared with me some of his notes. It was a very interesting hypothesis, and it involved more exploration before exploiting the intended product. When we went through the ideas of this book it became clear that my friend was falling into the Vannevar Bush "free play of the free intellect[29]" trap and he needed a more strict Moonshot attitude. It was also clear that the incentives were misaligned, and the scientist was closer to the HIV story we explored on paving a recognition path than to landing the Moonshot. Despite having invested for years, my friend decided to pull the plug, mostly due to his inability to manage this scientist. This is not an isolated case. In fact, I have found this struggle with businesses trying to manage scientists. It is not hard to create measurable scientific research results, but this is harder to create measurable scientific impact results. This struggle is about leveraging a scientist to *land* a Moonshot, having them working directly with company executives, elected politicians, due diligence teams or into operational management.

In many cases a scientist will likely be a research scientist, and turning them into an impact scientist is a gradual process over years and even over different jobs. I have collected some recommendations based on my own experience, and many interviews across fields, countries and fields of application:

Seek borders, cross boundaries. Test your skills developed in one field/place/topic into another one. It helps to see the value of the skills versus the knowledge. E.g. apply your image analysis skills of the sun on an Earth Observation image of the devastation of the hurricane to support response operations with better images. Use your experience making bacteria cultures to figure out how you could grow a plantation faster. I believe innovation can often be found across the interface or crossovers of knowledge or skills applied from one domain on different domains. Breaking assumptions is also another source of innovation, and crossing over to different domains can help identify and break assumptions.

What you built beats degrees on your curriculum. When hiring, organizations need an individual who will solve issues. *Their* issues. And they usually have little time and several candidates. Hiring is a substantial investment of time and effort, so in case of doubt, it is easy to pass. If potential hires can present a project they did from end to end, they are much keener to listen. Especially at the interview stage, an employer needs to know an employee can be useful on day one, not how many degrees or where you did them. Day one, and day "one hundred." This hundred-day test refers to the perceived ability of a new employee to be much more effective as it quickly learns on the first weeks and months. Pragmatically, degrees are more a presumption of skills, and ability to learn, than proof of applicable knowledge. More so when some of the most demanded skills are not part of official degrees, like data science.

Be humble; knowledge is less transferable than skills. Like the point above, I've have found especially difficult to accept that credentials, respect, and prominence in academia is based on very different set of rules as many other places. You might know what very few other academics know in the world, and might have worked in very selective places, but you will need to accept that you need to prove yourself again from scratch. Don't worry, if you are in the right place, your skills—more than your knowledge—will fast-track the process. It's not the fancy degree, it is the scientific ability to use those skills to absorb complexity and figure out a solution that will set you back on track.

Being critical ≠ being productive. Academics are good at finding and poking holes, at seeing if there is something wrong or weak, and what an ideal solution could be. Sometimes it is much better to focus on the balance of what already works and understand if that is enough for the scope of the purpose. This is especially important when working in teams, professional advice is important, but getting things done is better than doing things better. "Perfect is the enemy of good." Good enough is good enough, there will be time to make it better, if it makes sense.

Disagreeing is often the lazy excuse. There are many more ways to disagree than there are ways to a agree with something or someone. It is easier, an arguably intellectually lazier, to highlight a particular overlooked weakness and disagree. Yet progress generally depends on finding general agreement. Therefore, it is often harder to figure out how much agreement there is in the particular issue, and if that common ground is enough for the purpose of moving forward within the scope of the issue at the moment.

Learn to listen. Most people listen reactively. Most people do that most of the time. We listen thinking what to add to the conversation, so we tend to interrupt when we have something we feel is relevant enough. I believe this is a consequence of the critical thinking mentioned above. Learning to listen means listening along, paying attention, and not interrupting unless really needed. Sometimes words are bad conveyors of complex meaning, and it takes time to rightfully express oneself. Listening like this is harder than it seems, especially when the person talking is not as focused on facts as we researchers like to do.

Avoid paternalism. I have found that many scientists, myself included, fall into the trap of "I am the expert, so do what I say, because if you knew what I know, you would do what I say." Usually scientists might know part of the picture, but there are other perspectives to consider.

Even cases where the most appropriate thing to do is contrary to what the available data says. For instance, climate change, is not about just stopping the emissions of carbon dioxide by closing all factories right away. The issue is also about incentives, jobs, political agendas, diplomacy, etc. As much as scientist push out data arguing for the need to stop carbon emissions, progress is happening at venues where science is only part of the mix, such as within the United Nations or at the World Economic Forum in Davos.

Push less, pull more. This is something I've found with many formerly academic colleagues. We like to push from our knowledge, to explore the unknown, to understand. Often, we need the opposite. To pull from the solution to a problem. To start with the goal, like in the case of the Moonshot, and then backtrack what needs to happen until we can link to what we do today. Pulling from the end goal means making sure the output and the outcome are linked, it means there is less chance for pure exploration, but also draws a clear path of accountability. Having an explicit "pull" attitude in your projects, even research projects, helps reduce the risk of stagnation or the focus on the process itself. Same goes for communications, we tend to push a content when we communicate, when it is much more efficient to place yourself on the receiver side and think how to pull the content. This is especially important when speaking for example with policy makers, CEOs, or in general those who need to handle many dimensions at once when they also need to make decisions quickly.

Ask yourself if your goal is to create scientists or academics. Is the goal of your unit or department to apply science to create new knowledge, or to make scientists (people with skills in science, regardless of where they apply their expertise)? We tend to conflate that academia is the place where we make both things: academic research, and education of scientists. If you are creating scientists, build a measure of success that is not about number or papers, citations or funds given to the institution. Maybe it is based on pilot projects, or how many students are happily employed one year after graduation.

Think about mental health and well-being beyond managing crises. It is good to have a system to check on people and give professional help in crisis, but this also about teaching tools for mental health, resilience, stress management, introspection, and mindfulness on a continuous and ongoing basis. Several really good scientists I have worked with ended up suffering from mental health issues due to stress, anxiety, and other factors that ended their intended careers, and placing them in a future for which they were also unprepared for.

Measure happiness. I am a huge proponent of measuring happiness levels. Happiness is holistic, subjective, ill-defined, and partly a personal decision. This usually makes for a very poor indicator. However, lack of happiness usually happens for a concrete set of impediments one can work with. You can't be happy if you are very stressed, if you are sick, if you have an issue with your advisor, if your commute is two hours, if your grant didn't come through. Building a sense of happiness means working to remove the barriers that prevent people to seek happiness, especially those affecting the professional goals of your students.

Include soft skills in the training: Hire an expert to improve communications skills. A communications professional, by definition, is ideal, but someone like an actor, or a radio or TV anchor could give

111

really good insights. Create more public-facing student-organized events...

Provide visibility to non-research options. Contact companies and alumni to advertise their positions, internships or particular projects. Invite alumni who left academia to share their experience. Form alliances and agreements with other non-research institutions to share openings, news and conference opportunities. Break the assumption that the highest goal of science is to be an academic.

Provide mentors AND buddies. The figure of a mentor is important, as is someone with more professional experience to help you make decisions or work with concerns. Your PhD advisor is usually your mentor. The figure of a buddy is someone more of a fellow peer that has just been where you are, and so it can provide more personal and candid advice. A buddy could be a recent graduate or a post-doctoral student.

Address biases. Most scientists will come from academic backgrounds trained for research. Understand that their whole professional career they have been incentivized for excellence and abstraction, not timeliness. The incentive is trying to get the right data, in the right format, to address all cases at once, including edge cases, on a clean process. Not to deliver what is needed in a given time window. An academic scientist will get frustrated quickly when their workload is not academic, and has to deal with a forced limited scope, a concrete staged timeline of results, or has to handle soft skills. Communicate and work on these biases early on.

Leverage on skills. Academic scientists are, by training, fast learners. Their education was based on tools to absorb complexity and novelty. Therefore, shadowing, and high cadence of rotation on the first few days can work really well. This means having them just sit next to a more experienced colleague and have them ask questions as the work is being done. Rotating quickly on the first few days also helps get a comprehensive picture of the workload and implications, much more than focusing on the in-depth technical details of their particular workload. In fact, one of their bias will probably be to tend to go down the rabbit hole of increasingly particular and detailed implications of a specific problem, rather than getting just deep enough to solve the problem, or defer the decision to go deeper only if it makes sense to spend the time.

Round up skills. An academic scientist is very asymmetrically trained. They might be able to master very specific and valuable skills, but might be unable to present that value to others in an internal event, or be minimally effective at a client or stakeholder meeting. Addressing those asymmetries directly with concrete milestones will speed up the process into a much more effective team member.

Manage pulling from solutions, not pushing from principles. Scientists are trained to start from (falsifiable) principles or hypothesis, and then move towards the goal from there. In goal oriented practical settings there are several problems with this approach. For one, principles are most times idealistic conditions than might not include variables than yield the approach ill-defined, biased, or blind to important aspects. When managing from the goal, and pulling from what is needed, we are forced to consider all aspects, and in a way that they bring it closer to the goal, it also prevents secondary findings which might be interesting but not conductive to the goal. It also makes it easier to budget time, resources, and potential problems. Pulling from the goals is saying "What do you need so I can get this done by this date" instead of "What do you think about this issue? How can we fix it?"

What would you do?

Another practical way to explain the value of impact science that I have used on my workshops and courses is to explore pragmatism and impact via hypothetical scenarios. Some situations have a clear answer, some not, but in either case, it helps exemplify the rounding up of skills highlighted on the previous section.

The celebrity boost

In the summer of 2018, I had the chance to visit a very important international research institution on climate change and the environment. The group I was with included some other fellow scientists but interestingly it also included "media celebrities" and award-winning journalists from major international newspapers. People with truly tens of millions of followers who trust them in social media. People whose every online update is instantly read, shared, and commented on. If we want impact with science, it is an interesting and relevant question how scientist could or should relate with that kind of power. For example, should some scientists become media celebrities? How do we partner with them to help drive this impact?.

The director of the research institution we were visiting gave a not-so-short speech about the kind of research that was done there: Many nations present, many open questions to research, many important papers, doctorates, and research ongoing around us. Very interesting indeed, but probably with a bit too much detail for some of the audience. A journalist from a major international newspaper, jumped with the golden question of this hypothetical scenario: "If you could share a simple message with the world to help improve the situation, what would it be?" Indeed. This is a question many researchers get when they are interviewed in the context of an important discovery, or around a public outreach talk. Having also media celebrities on the room, made me think even deeper about this scenario. Between journalists and researchers there tends to be a natural tension between the scientist wanting factual reporting with all nuisances and caveats, and the journalist wanting a succinct clear headline that will be read, and cared, by everyone.

With celebrities and the so-called influencers, there might even be a bigger tension with scientists. In the traditional image of research and academia, facts are the light of progress. Hard learned tools of research leading to hard earned facts. The more facts one can uncover, the better we are. Facts carry their own weight, and fact are enough. If only more people knew them, the world would be better. Therefore, either you should discover the facts for yourself thereby becoming an expert, or otherwise non-experts should just listen to experts so that we all knew better and can be better. This paternalistic approach is the "information deficit" hypothesis most scientists assume truth. For celebrities the model is radically different: paying attention has a high cost, especially around topics one doesn't care at first. We seek to associate with others we can trust, we identify with, or would like to. In essence, we seek to belong to groups of common identity, real or desired. Moreover, given the cost of attention and thinking, we are naturally good at choosing to make decisions with as little information as possible. For that we use assumptions, heuristics, stereotyping, or we follow what the leader says. This is sometimes called the "low-information rationality" hypothesis, and while extremely common and effective, it is dangerous since it disfavors fact-based reasoning. Yet, we all have a set of famous people we follow, care, and listen to. The somewhat uncomfortable reality is that an influencer or celebrity post reaches, and indeed influences, within seconds an audience that the most important *Nature* article will never reach. One might argue that it is as important to generate knowledge as it is to have it known and acted upon by as many people as possible. This is partly why organizations like the UN or the EU have "Goodwill ambassadors" to promote children's rights and use the notability of these celebrities to drive media and political attention. These include Antonio Banderas for UNDP, Shakira for the UN, Messi for UNICEF or Angelina Jolie for UNHCR[30].

Here is another case to validate this hypothesis. On one side, running with the "information deficit hypothesis" a group of researchers tried different methods to explain why vaccines are important. In experiment, published in 2014 in the journal *Pediatrics*[31], they tried explaining vaccine facts, debunking the hoax relationship between vaccines and autism, explaining the disease or the details of a particular unvaccinated kids who almost died. None of these approaches increased the perception of value for vaccines. On the other hand, while describing this paper[32], the science journalist Pere Estupinyá confronts it with the experience of a famous doctor that in her family office is able to change the perception and behavior of their patients. It is again trust in the doctor more than trust in the science what drives people to change, or not, their opinion of a scientific issue.

Back to our case, the director of this research institution we were visiting, when asked about what he would say on climate change to millions of people, his answer was:

"Don't trust what anyone says, including me. Make your own conclusions."

Squarely hitting the target on the "information deficit" hypothesis scientists tend to follow, and oblivious to the "low-information rationality" hypothesis celebrities tend to follow. I truly don't know what I would say, and I believe it is a good exercise to think about this case, or more in general how we can leverage the power of facts and fame, how they interact or can they work together. May be the answer is closer to a succinct phrase that hits both targets of low-information rational and hints towards learning more. I don't know the answer for climate change, but in nutrition, I believe Michael Pollan hits the right spot with his book *In Defense of Food*[33]. The whole book tries to drive this narrow space between pragmatic advice and critical thinking, and he explicitly addressed the point of this section on his first phrase, with an advice that summarized the book: *"Eat food, not too much, mostly plants."* The rest of the book is dedicated to unfolding this phrase into logic, research, facts, history, and recommendations. He, too, could have said about food, "Don't trust what anyone says, including me. Make your own conclusions," but that phrase gives both concrete direction easy to follow and nudges the reader to want to know more.

Back again to our research director, after the rounds of questions about climate change research and impact, and his answers, I approached him, and I told him about the idea of impact science, about the fact that some in the room were celebrities, and a little bit about what I described here on leveraging their reach. His refined answer was, "Diversity, we need diversity in the world, and if we are not careful, we will lose it." I like this answer more, and so did the celebrity I talked to afterwards. Still, she didn´t post it on her channels. I don´t know what I would say, but it would probably be something like: "There is no *away* when you throw away, the smoke that goes up, comes down somewhere else. Reduce what you use, avoid plastics, recycle, choose the better option." I would try to make it concrete, to make it relatable and to hint to the reason so you can learn more. I am sure there are better way to say it. My question is then for you. Think of the most famous person you follow, and think of an issue where science has a lot to offer. Imagine this famous person gives you their platform to say something. What would you say to millions of people?

Mr. President, this is what you will do

Often, when we look for impact we look at our leaders, our presidents, head of state or elected politicians. They are seen as the enabler or blocker to action, especially in issues like climate change. As I explained on previous chapters there is huge, and growing, pile of academic evidence that the global climate system is disrupted by our actions, and we must change course. On my talks I often start with this hypothetical scenario. You are sitting down with your heads of state, or your city major. Think personally of them and of you, not a hypothetical unknown leader. It might a very progressive democratic leader, or the impulsive dictator of your country. You happen to be on the table in the morning and she or him turns to you and says, "What do I do?" and you answer, *"This is what I think you should do: ..."*

Depending on where you are from, the baggage that comes with this question is very different. Maybe you live on a very intense car culture, or there are big factories around, or your electricity comes from burning gas or coal, or the opposition leader is a climate change denier, or there is really no budget left for expensive new programs.

You cannot tell them to read the latest papers, or the latest hefty IPCC synthesis report with hundreds of pages or general recommendations. If you are on the table with them, it is probably your job to read it, absorb it and then come up with solutions. Depending on your location, it might easier of harder to figure out what kind of action they should embark on, but what is very clear is that this advice better considers all those aspects of finance, politics, strategy. You can write them down, think of the possible counter responses for your particular location. This hopefully uncomfortable meeting is exactly the kind of process an impact scientist should face, in this case helping translate the academic findings into policy on the ground. There should be tensions, disagreement, no easy answers, and hard challenges in the process. Furthermore, the most important moment is probably when there are things that are academically needed but the leader chooses not to do. In the end it is their role and responsibility to decide, not yours. Your role then is to accept this and, if possible, understand why, so next time we can present a better solution that can be implemented.

When I was at the World Bank, I had a meeting with its president around our approach for an upcoming key event. I presented my advice, he heard it, and he told me he disagreed for a set of reasons he mentioned. I tried to push back, but he told me not to, the decision was taken. I needed to accept it and reflect on the decision. He was kind to explain the reasons, he doesn't need to, and may there were others he didn't mention, but somewhere there was something I was not understanding or not seeing. Either way, my role is then to accept it, incorporate the decision into the general approach and move on. This is what we did and we kept working and agreeing on other aspects. In the private sector, this is sometimes called "disagree and commit." You should voice your disagreement, but then you should also be able to commit to the executive decision even when it is not the way you would do it. In academia, disagreement is stubborn. We are encouraged to debate so we can find the root of it, and either agree or find ways to solve the disagreement. When leaders make decisions, they can have huge impact, and whether they were right or wrong have many more dimensions than objective data or academic debate. In these cases, it is both important and difficult to offer our most reality grounded advice for that particular scope, more than it is to be academically correct.

So, in your local context, for the particular issue at hand, complete the phrase: *"Dear President, this is what I think you should do: ..."*

Index

Book Endnotes

[1] It's a known fact that the retreat is because of the effects of climate change. https://www.researchgate.net/profile/Andreas_Vieli/publication/235640596_Large-scale_changes_in_Greenland_outlet_glacier_dynamics_triggered_at_the_terminus/links/54200b420cf241a65a1afaf0/Large-scale-changes-in-Greenland-outlet-glacier-dynamics-triggered-at-the-terminus.pdf

[2] It's more than just breath ancient air, the bubbles gives us a lot of information about evolution of the ice and its history. https://www.cambridge.org/core/services/aop-cambridge-core/content/view/207477CB49617C926A111C331AA69F4A/S002214300001279Xa.pdf/significance_of_air_bubbles_in_glacier_ice.pdf

[3] The documentary "Bending the arch" depicts this progress, from setting the organization to when he joined the World Bank Group as president. https://en.wikipedia.org/wiki/Bending_the_Arc

[4] http://foreignpolicy.com/2016/04/27/is-jim-yong-kim-destroying-the-world-bank-development-finance/

[5] The original paper describing the business model and several potential areas for implementation was published in 2016, and available here https://www.sciencedirect.com/science/article/pii/S0308597X16300586 Enric has also spoken about the concept on several Ted talks and interviews.

[6] The phrase, coined in 1994, refers to much more than profit and loss, to full cost accounting. http://www.johnelkington.com/archive/TBL-elkington-chapter.pdf

[7] Bhutan is a small community with a strong national identity and union. This means that, despite long windy roads and times to connect across the country, communities are closely united. My experience was that everyone knew someone in the region or place you were asking about for the mapping exercise; or the knew exactly who to call. As way of reference, this is reflected e.g. on this interview about soccer https://www.npr.org/2015/03/17/393646668/bhutan-one-step-closer-to-world-cup-after-shocking-victory-over-sri-lanka?t=1535798543478

[8] There are many reported cases of misuse of mosquito nets used for fishing, not only around the Malawi lake, but also other regions. This is a good summary of the situation, in 2016 https://e360.yale.edu/features/misuse-of-malaria-fighting-mosquito-nets-stressing-lake-malawi-fish-populations

[9] https://www.amazon.com/Fourth-Industrial-Revolution-Klaus-Schwab-ebook/dp/B01JEMROIU

[10] See article on the scurvy here, and references therein: https://dash.harvard.edu/bitstream/handle/1/8852139/Mayberry.html

[11] The time of HIV/AIDS cases is a well-researched topic, with many nuisances and complexities, like the different types of HIV, the effect of public policies, the inter-relation with the socio-economic, cultural and political factors of each country. For

this part I based my research in sources quoted on Wikipedia articles, this article about relation of gay sexual practices https://www.ncbi.nlm.nih.gov/pubmed/8030625 . the book "The Band Played on" and this article about possible sources of the USA being hit particularly hard and fast: https://newrepublic.com/article/117691/aids-hit-united-states-harder-other-developed-countries-why

[12] Estimates for how many people received contaminated Factor VIII range substantially, and also across many countries. This also includes spreading of other diseases, like Hepatitis C. References to estimates and disputes around these cases can be found e.g. here: https://en.wikipedia.org/wiki/Contaminated_haemophilia_blood_products#cite_note-NYTimes1996-1

[13] You can hear here the cut of when it happened: https://thescene.com/watch/vanityfair/the-reagan-administration-s-chilling-response-to-the-aids-crisis?source=player_scene_logo

[14] Francis, Donald P. "Deadly AIDS policy failure by the highest levels of the US government: A personal look back 30 years later for lessons to respond better to future epidemics." *Journal of Public Health Policy* 33 (2012): 290-300.

[15]

https://www.amazon.com/gp/search?index=books&linkCode=qs&keywords=9780226020495

[16]https://www.amazon.com/Scientific-Errors-Controversies-U-S-Epidemic/dp/0313347174/ref=sr_1_1?s=books&ie=UTF8&qid=1529509074&sr=1-1&keywords=9780313347177

[17] https://www.amazon.com/Gray-Rhino-Recognize-Obvious-Dangers/dp/125005382X

[18] You can find some names here http://fortune.com/2017/07/10/climate-change-green-house-gases/

[19] In May 2017 Nature published a study on the detection of increasing CFC-11 with unknown origin. This is still research in progress and unknown if the source CFC is newly made or the leakage of stored appliances, but the findings are conclusive of an increased emission in the recent years that. https://www.nature.com/articles/s41586-018-0106-2.epdf

[20] For a more detailed view of the effectiveness of the Kyoto Protocol see e.g. this "New Scientist" article, accessed on May 2018 https://www.newscientist.com/article/2093579-was-kyoto-climate-deal-a-success-figures-reveal-mixed-results/

[21] The good news of reduced child mortality across the World is one of the key messages Dr. Hans Rossling became famous for. For more context-setting and the relation with education and development in general, his TED talk is a good pointer for more information: [Accessed in May,2018] https://www.ted.com/talks/hans_rosling_the_good_news_of_the_decade

[22] https://www.ted.com/talks/jane_chen_a_warm_embrace_that_saves_lives

124

[23] At the time of the acquisition, the so-called deep artificial intelligence applied on images was on its earliest stages. Today these features are much common. I learned about the backstory of Magic Pony and how it came to be from one of the VC funders, and was widely reported in 2016: https://techcrunch.com/2016/06/20/twitter-is-buying-magic-pony-technology-which-uses-neural-networks-to-improve-images/

[24] See http://www.druidcollective.org/ or the presentation of the work with Mark Pollock in this video https://www.youtube.com/watch?v=MFuEfK54OEE

[25] https://www.patientslikeme.com/ and https://www.rareconnect.org/en

[26] There are several reports on this "The Millennial Effect", this report from Capgemini is one of them: https://www.capgemini.com/2016/06/the-millennial-effect/

[27] https://www.nytimes.com/2013/12/30/technology/solving-problems-for-real-world-using-design.html

[28] "How to change the world" happens every year, and I met, and accessed the website, in 2018: https://www.ucl.ac.uk/steapp/steapp-news-publication/2017/750-students-65-experts-5-challenges

[29] https://www.nsf.gov/od/lpa/nsf50/vbush1945.htm

[30] The list of Goodwill ambassadors for e.g. UNICEF: https://en.wikipedia.org/wiki/List_of_UNICEF_Goodwill_Ambassadors

[31] "Effective Messages in Vaccine Promotion: A Randomized Trial". Brendan Nyhan, Jason Reifler, Sean Richey and Gary L. Freed. Pediatrics. April 2014, 133 (4) e835-e842; DOI: https://doi.org/10.1542/peds.2013-2365

[32] "A vivir la Ciencia" is a Spanish book written by Pere Estupinyá. He recalls and reflects the experience of being the host of one of science section at the radio sation with the most audience in Spain "A vivir". The reference I make is on page 113.

[33] https://www.amazon.com/gp/product/0143114964/ref=dbs_a_def_rwt_bibl_vppi_i2

Made in the USA
Middletown, DE
21 August 2021

46059357R00070